1 & 2 TIMOTHY

Passing the Torch

LifeWay | Small Groups

Group Directory

Pass this Directory around and have your Group Members
fill in their names and phone numbers

Name   **Phone**

_____   _____

_____   _____

_____   _____

_____   _____

_____   _____

_____   _____

_____   _____

_____   _____

_____   _____

_____   _____

_____   _____

_____   _____

_____   _____

_____   _____

1 & 2 TIMOTHY

Passing the Torch

EDITING AND PRODUCTION TEAM:
James F. Couch, Jr., Lyman Coleman, Sharon Penington,
Cathy Tardif, Christopher Werner, Matthew Lockhart,
Richard Peace, Erika Tiepel, Andrew Sloan,
Edgar C. Mills, Gregory C. Benoit,
Margaret Harris, Scott Lee

NASHVILLE, TENNESSEE

Passing the Torch: A Study on Leadership from 1 & 2 Timothy
© 1988, 1998, 2003 Serendipity House
Seventh Printing 2013

Published by Serendipity House Publishers
Nashville, Tennessee

ISBN: 978-1-5749-4325-2
Item: 001197655

To purchase additional copies of this resource or other studies:
ORDER ONLINE at www.SerendipityHouse.com
WRITE Serendipity House, One LifeWay Plaza, Nashville, TN 37234-0152
FAX (615) 251-5933

1-800-458-2772
www.SerendipityHouse.com

Printed in the United States of America

Table of Contents

Core Values

Community:
: The purpose of this curriculum is to build community within the body of believers around Jesus Christ.

Group Process:
: To build community, the curriculum must be designed to take a group through a step-by-step process of sharing your story with one another.

Interactive Bible Study:
: To share your "story," the approach to Scripture in the curriculum needs to be open-ended and right brain—to "level the playing field" and encourage everyone to share.

Developmental Stages:
: To provide a healthy program throughout the four stages of the life cycle of a group, the curriculum needs to offer courses on three levels of commitment: (1) Beginner Level—low-level entry, high structure, to level the playing field; (2) Growth Level—deeper Bible study, flexible structure, to encourage group accountability; (3) Discipleship Level—in-depth Bible study, open structure, to move the group into high gear.

Target Audiences:
: To build community throughout the culture of the church, the curriculum needs to be flexible, adaptable and transferable into the structure of the average church.

Mission:
: To expand the Kingdom of God one person at a time by filling the "empty chair." (We add an extra chair to each group session to remind us of our mission.)

Introduction

Each healthy small group will move through various stages as it matures.

Growth Stage: Here the group begins to care for one another as it learns to apply what they learn through Bible study, worship and prayer.

Develop Stage: The inductive Bible study deepens while the group members discover and develop gifts and skills. The group explores ways to invite their neighbors and coworkers to group meetings.

Birth Stage: This is the time in which group members form relationships and begin to develop community. The group will spend more time in ice-breaker exercises, relational Bible study and covenant building.

Multiply Stage: The group begins the multiplication process. Members pray about their involvement in new groups. The "new" groups begin the life cycle again with the Birth Stage.

Subgrouping: If you have nine or more people at a meeting, Serendipity recommends you divide into subgroups of 3–6 for the Bible study. Ask one person to be the leader of each subgroup and to follow the directions for the Bible study. After 30 minutes, the Group Leader will call "time" and ask all subgroups to come together for the Caring Time.

Each group meeting should include all parts of the "three-part agenda."

 Ice-Breaker: Fun, history-giving questions are designed to warm the group and to build understanding about the other group members. You can choose to use all of the Ice-Breaker questions, especially if there is a new group member that will need help in feeling comfortable with the group.

 Bible Study: The heart of each meeting is the reading and examination of the Bible. The questions are open, discover questions that lead to further inquiry. Reference notes are provided to give everyone a "level playing field." The emphasis is on understanding what the Bible says and applying the truth to real life. The questions for each session build. There is always at least one "going deeper" question provided. You should always leave time for the last of the "questions for interaction." Should you choose, you can use the optional "going deeper" question to satisfy the desire for the challenging questions in groups that have been together for a while.

 Caring Time: All study should point us to actions. Each session ends with prayer and direction in caring for the needs of the group members. You can choose between several questions. You should always pray for the "empty chair." Who do you know that could fill that void in your group?

Sharing Your Story: These sessions are designed for members to share a little of their personal lives each time. Through a number of special techniques each member is encouraged to move from low risk, less personal sharing to higher risk responses. This helps develop the sense of community and facilitates caregiving.

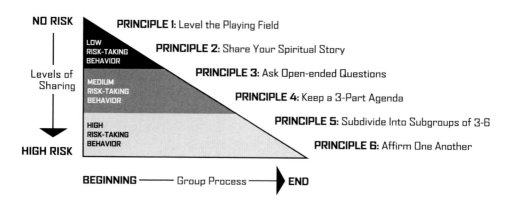

Group Covenant: A group covenant is a "contract" that spells out your expectations and the ground rules for your group. It's very important that your group discuss these issues—preferably as part of the first session.

GROUND RULES:

- Priority: While you are in the group, you give the group meeting priority.

- Participation: Everyone participates and no one dominates.

- Respect: Everyone is given the right to their own opinion and all questions are encouraged and respected.

- Confidentiality: Anything that is said in the meeting is never repeated outside the meeting.

- Empty Chair: The group stays open to new people at every meeting.

- Support: Permission is given to call upon each other in time of need—even in the middle of the night.

- Advice Giving: Unsolicited advice is not allowed.

- Mission: We agree to do everything in our power to start a new group as our mission.

ISSUES:

- The time and place this group is going to meet is_____

- Refreshments are _____ responsibility.

- Child care is _____ responsibility.

Ten Steps for Multiplying Small Groups

1. **Share a vision:** From the very first meeting of a group the vision must be cast for the mission. God can greatly affect the larger body of Christ through a small group if there is a vision for creating new groups and bringing people into the kingdom. If the group will make a group covenant that envisions multiplying into new groups, then new groups will happen. An effective leader will regularly keep this goal in front of the group. It is essential to raise up group leaders from your group and to divide into new groups every 18-24 months. Announce the intention to multiply early and often.

2. **Building a new leadership team:** As the group matures through the Growth and Develop Stages, the present leadership team should identify apprentice leaders and facilitators. This is done best in a small group setting. Look for an engineer type as the group administrator, the party animal as the hospitality person, a person that loves interaction and knowledge as the facilitator and a caring person to handle group shepherding. Next you must seek to train and mentor them as they grow in confidence. Here is an outline of this process:

    a. Identify apprentice leaders and facilitators
    b. Provide on-the-job training
    c. Give them the opportunity to lead your group
    d. Introduce the new team to your church
    e. Launch the new group

3. **Determine the type of group:** Who are you trying to reach? Here are four commonly identified audiences.

Group		Percentage	Group Type
a.	Core	10%	Discipleship Group
b.	Congregation	30%	Pulpit or Care Groups
c.	Crowd	60%	Felt Need Groups
d.	Seekers	Outsiders	Support Groups
e.		All	Affinity Groups
f.		All	Covenant Groups

4. **Conduct a Felt Need Survey:** Use either a custom survey for your church or the one included in this book to determine an area or a specific topic for your first study.

5. **Choose curriculum:** Make sure your choice fits the group type and the stage in the life cycle of your group. All Serendipity courses are pre-selected for stage of the life cycle.

6. **Ask someone to serve as host:** Determine when and where the group will meet. Someone must coordinate the following.

    a. Where the meeting will be held.
    b. Who will provide babysitters (if necessary).
    c. Who will teach children (if necessary).
    d. Who will provide refreshments.

7. **Find out who will go with the new team**: There are several options in beginning new groups.

    a. Encourage several members of your group to go with the new leadership team to start a new group.
    b. The existing leadership team will leave to start a new group leaving the existing group with the new team.
    c. Several groups can break off beginning all new groups.

8. **Begin countdown**: Use a study designed to help multiply groups, building each week until you launch your new group.

9. **Celebrate**: Have a party with presents for the new group. Make announcements to your church, advertising the new group and its leadership team.

10. **Keep casting a vision**: Remember as you start new groups to keep casting a vision for multiplying into new groups.

Leadership Team for Small Groups

Coordinator: Is responsible to the church leadership team for:
1. Building a leadership team.
2. Ensuring the coordination of the group.
3. Meeting with the leadership team once a month for encouragement and planning.
4. Casting a vision for multiplication and beginning the process of multiplication.

Facilitating Team: Is responsible to the coordinator for:
1. Guiding the group in life-changing Bible study.
2. Developing a facilitating team for subgrouping into groups of three to six.
3. Keeping the group on agenda, but being sensitive when someone needs to share.
4. Subdividing the group for Bible study and caring time and emphasizing the "empty chair."

Care Team: Is responsible to the coordinator for:
1. Contacting group members to encourage attendance and personal growth.
2. Keeping the group informed of prayer needs.
3. Coordinating caring for the special needs of the group.

Party Team: Is responsible to the coordinator for:
1. Planning, coordinating and promoting monthly group parties.
2. Keeping the members involved in the party activities.

Host/Hostess: Is responsible to the coordinator for:
1. Providing a clean home with enough space to subdivide into groups of three to six.
2. Coordinating refreshments.
3. Welcoming guests and having name tags at each meeting.
4. Making sure everything is conducive for sharing (no TV, comfortable temperature, arrangements for children).

Felt Need Survey

Types of Studies that I find most interesting:
- ❏ Issues about spiritual development, such as learning to love like God does or knowing God's will.
- ❏ Studying about Jesus Christ.
- ❏ Issues about personal development, such as managing stress or understanding the stages of growth in marriage.
- ❏ Learning about the major truths of the Christian faith.
- ❏ Studying the teaching of the apostle Paul.
- ❏ Working through specific areas personal struggle, such as coping with teenagers or handling a death in the family.
- ❏ Learning about the books of the New Testament other than the gospels and epistles of Paul.

Rank the following factor in order of importance to you with 1 being the highest and five being the lowest:
- _____ The passage of Scripture that is being studied.
- _____ The topic or issue that is being discussed.
- _____ The affinity of group members (age, vocation, interest).
- _____ The mission of the group (service projects, evangelism, starting groups).
- _____ Personal encouragement.

Rank the following spiritual development needs in order of interest to you with 1 being the highest and 5 being the lowest:
- _____ Learning how to become a follower of Christ.
- _____ Gaining a basic understanding of the truths of the faith.
- _____ Improving my disciplines of devotion, prayer, reading Scripture.
- _____ Gaining a better knowledge of what is in the Bible.
- _____ Applying the truths of Scripture to my life.

Of the various studies below check the appropriate boxes that indicate: if you would be interested in studying for your personal needs (P), you think would be helpful for your group (G), or you have friends that are not in the groups that would come to a group studying this subject (F).

Understanding the Savior (13-week studies)	P	G	F
Mark 1-8: Jesus, the Early Years	❏	❏	❏
Mark 8-16: Jesus, the Final Days	❏	❏	❏
John 12-21: The Passion of the Son	❏	❏	❏
The Miracles of Jesus	❏	❏	❏
The Life of Christ	❏	❏	❏

The Message of Paul

	P	G	F
Romans 1-7: Who We Really Are (13 weeks)	☐	☐	☐
Romans 8-16: Being a Part of God's Plan (13 weeks)	☐	☐	☐
1 Corinthians: Taking on Tough Issues (13 weeks)	☐	☐	☐
Galatians: Living by Grace (13 weeks)	☐	☐	☐
Ephesians: Together in Christ (12 weeks)	☐	☐	☐
Philippians: Running the Race (7 weeks)	☐	☐	☐

Words of Faith

Acts 1-14: The Church on Fire (13 weeks)	☐	☐	☐
Acts 15-28: The Irrepressible Witness (13 weeks)	☐	☐	☐
Hebrews: Jesus Through the Eyes of Hebrew Faith (13 weeks)	☐	☐	☐
James: Faith at Work (12 weeks)	☐	☐	☐
1 Peter: Staying the Course (10 weeks)	☐	☐	☐
1 John: Walking in the Light (11 weeks)	☐	☐	☐
Revelation 1-12: End of Time (13 weeks)	☐	☐	☐
Revelation 13-22: The New Jerusalem (13 weeks)	☐	☐	☐

301 Bible Studies with Home Work Assignments (13-week studies)

Ephesians: Our Riches in Christ	☐	☐	☐
James: Walking the Talk	☐	☐	☐
Life of Christ: Behold the Man	☐	☐	☐
Parables: Virtual Reality	☐	☐	☐
Philippians: Joy under Stress	☐	☐	☐
Sermon on the Mount: Examining Your Life	☐	☐	☐
1 John: The Test of Faith	☐	☐	☐

Women of Purpose Series (6-week studies)

Faith Untamed	☐	☐	☐
Forever Touched: Significant Women in Jesus' Life	☐	☐	☐
Held in High Esteem: Women Commended by Paul	☐	☐	☐
Famine to Fairy Tale: Ruth & Naomi's Path to Redemption	☐	☐	☐
Redeeming Our Regrets: The Entangled Lives of Sarah & Hagar	☐	☐	☐

Men of Purpose Series

Hope Under Construction: Nehemiah (12 weeks)	☐	☐	☐
Fearless Leadership: Joshua (12 weeks)	☐	☐	☐
Becoming a Catalyst: Paul (12 weeks)	☐	☐	☐
Shoulder to Shoulder: The Apostles (12 weeks)	☐	☐	☐
Unwavering Tenacity: Elijah (12 weeks)	☐	☐	☐
Empowered by God: Moses (13 weeks)	☐	☐	☐
Overcoming Adversity: Insights Into the Life of Jonah (12 weeks)	☐	☐	☐
Weighting Anchor: Samuel (13 weeks)	☐	☐	☐

Life Connections Series (Unique series blends master-teacher larger group format with effective small-group encounters: 13-week studies)

	P	G	F
Essential Truth: Knowing Christ Personally	❑	❑	❑
Vital Pursuits: Developing My Spiritual Life	❑	❑	❑
Authentic Relationships: Being Real in an Artificial World	❑	❑	❑
Unique Design: Connecting with the Christian Community	❑	❑	❑
Acts: Model for Today's Church	❑	❑	❑
Critical Decisions: Surviving in Today's World	❑	❑	❑
Intentional Choices: Discovering Contentment in Stressful Times	❑	❑	❑
Unleashed Influence: Power of Servant Leadership	❑	❑	❑
Proverbs: Uncommon Sense	❑	❑	❑
Contagious Community: Living Beyond Yourself	❑	❑	❑
1 & 2 Samuel: Heart of a Renegade King	❑	❑	❑
Lasting Legacy: Making a Difference with My Life	❑	❑	❑
Hosea to Malachi: Twelve Timeless Voices	❑	❑	❑
1 & 2 Thessalonians: Return of the King	❑	❑	❑

Warning Against False Teachers

Scripture 1 Timothy 1:1–11

The apostle Paul was most likely the author of 1 and 2 Timothy. Most agree that 1 Timothy was written about A.D. 63–65.

The theme of this letter is faithful ministry. The apostle Paul gives Timothy and the Ephesian elders the command to watch their lives and doctrine closely.

When Paul met Timothy, he was living in Lystra, in the Roman province of Galatia (which is modern Turkey). Timothy's mother was Jewish (Acts 16:1) and his father was a Gentile (a person of non-Jewish descent or religion). Timothy, his mother Eunice and grandmother Lois were. By the time of Paul's second visit to the area, Timothy was mature enough in the faith that the local church recommended Timothy to Paul as one who would be a helpful traveling companion (Acts 16:2). Paul decided that Timothy needed to be circumcised first, to convince Paul's Jewish critics of Timothy's eligibility to minister. If Timothy remained uncircumcised, these critics would identify Timothy with his Greek father, rather than his Jewish mother. Apparently Paul thought this Jewish rite was essential for Timothy's ministry, even though Paul clearly did not consider circumcision necessary for salvation (Acts 15).

The letters in the New Testament give clarification to who Timothy was and his relationship to the apostle Paul. He was a coworker with the apostle (Rom. 16:21; 1 Cor. 16:10; Phil. 2:22; 1 Thess. 3:2), and he worked with Paul in the writing of six of his letters (1 and 2 Thess.; 2 Cor.; Phil.; Col.; Philem.). Timothy was more than just a colleague; Paul considered him a beloved friend. He referred to him as "who is my beloved and faithful child in the Lord" (1 Cor. 4:17). In Philippians 2:20–22 the aging apostle writes, "For I have no one else like-minded ... . But you know his proven character, because he has served with me in the gospel ministry like a son with a father."

The Pastoral Epistles (the letters to Timothy and Titus) are set apart from the other letters by Paul because these three epistles address people and not churches. Although there are several personal remarks to Timothy himself, the main part of the letter directs him in his task of establishing sound teaching (1:18–19; 4:6–16; 6:11–21). A possible reason for the lack of intimate communication with Timothy is that the letter is not only intended for the young man but also for the church. Paul needs the church to know that he has given Timothy the authority to deal with the "false teachers" and the turmoil they are causing.

Welcome to this study of 1 and 2 Timothy! Together we will find inspiration and wisdom to help us carry out our ministry in life. We will be encouraged to defend the truth at all times and to stand up for our beliefs.

Exactly what false teaching that was being encountered in the church at Ephesus is not clear. It seems that the controversy revolved around some principles (doctrine) that were not based on accepted Christian teaching. This questionable speculation was probably conceived in private and confidential settings with no accountability to the authority of the apostles and their teaching.

It is possible that this false teaching was coming from within the church by some of the elders. It is clear that the elders were doing the teaching in Ephesus (3:2; 5:17), and Paul points out that those who are troubling the church are "teachers" (1:3,7; 6:3). He devotes a good portion of the letter to outlining the qualifications for leaders of a church, not only to establish church order but to respond to the elders of the Ephesian church who have strayed from sound teaching. These qualifications stand in sharp contrast to what is known about these false teachers.

These false teachers "forbid marriage" (4:3). Paul on the other hand writes that elders "must be husbands of one wife, managing their children and their own households competently" (3:12; see also 3:2, 4–5). These elders believe "that godliness is a way to material gain" (6:5); yet the apostle says, an elder must be "not greedy for money" (3:3). In other words, Paul is saying, "Here are the qualifications of true elders—in contrast to those who have strayed." He then outlines a process of selection, discipline and replacement of elders "who sin" (5:20).

 Ice-Breaker Connect With Your Group (15 minutes)

Today we are beginning a journey together by studying how the apostle Paul confronted false teachers and wrong beliefs about God. Before we look into the passage let's spend some time getting to know each other by sharing answers to the following questions.

Leader
Be sure to read the introductory material in the front of this book prior to this first session. To help your group members get acquainted, have each person introduce him or herself and then take turns answering one or two of the Ice-Breaker questions. If time allows, you may want to discuss all three questions.

1. When you were growing up, what did your dad do for a living? What did your mom do?

2. How do you react when you get lost?

    ○ I panic!
    ○ I adapt to my surroundings.
    ○ I have a melt down.
    ○ It doesn't bother me at all.
    ○ Being lost is an adventure.
    ○ I am a little apprehensive, but I overcome.
    ○ I have the confidence that I can handle anything.
    ○ I never get lost.
    ○ Other _____.

3. Describe a time in your life when you were really lost. What caused you to get lost? Is there a way to get lost that is not just physical disorientation? Has that ever happened to you?

 Bible Study Read Scripture and Discuss (30 minutes)

After a warm and encouraging greeting, Paul immediately warns Timothy and the church at Ephesus about those who are teaching false doctrines. He explains how this can cause controversy and distract people from God's plan of love and faith. Read 1 Timothy 1:1–11 and note how Paul describes the purpose of the Law.

Leader
Select a member of the group ahead of time to read aloud the Scripture passage. Then discuss the Questions for Interaction, dividing into subgroups of three to six. Allow everyone in the subgroup an opportunity to answer the questions. Don't forget to save time at the end for the Caring Time.

Warning Against False Teachers

1 Paul, an apostle of Christ Jesus according to the command of God our Savior and of Christ Jesus, our hope:
²To Timothy, my true child in the faith.
Grace, mercy, and peace from God the Father and Christ Jesus our Lord.
³As I urged you when I went to Macedonia, remain in Ephesus so that you may command certain people not to teach other doctrine ⁴or to pay attention to myths and endless genealogies. These promote empty speculations rather than God's plan, which operates by faith. ⁵Now the goal of our instruction is love from a pure heart, a good conscience, and a sincere faith. ⁶Some have deviated from these and turned aside to fruitless discussion. ⁷They want to be teachers of the law, although they don't understand what they are saying or what they are insisting on. ⁸Now we know that the law is good, provided one uses it legitimately. ⁹We know that the law is not meant for a righteous person, but for the lawless and rebellious, for the ungodly and sinful, for the unholy and irreverent, for those who kill their fathers and mothers, for murderers, ¹⁰for the sexually immoral and homosexuals, for kidnappers, liars, perjurers, and for whatever else is contrary to the sound teaching ¹¹based on the glorious gospel of the blessed God that was entrusted to me.

1 Timothy 1:1–11

Questions for Interaction

Leader
Refer to the Summary and Study Notes at the end of this session as needed. If 30 minutes is not enough time to answer all of the questions in this section, conclude the Bible Study by answering questions 6 and 7.

1. How would you feel if you were asked to deal with false doctrine and speculation that was being taught in the church? How would you handle the situation?

2. Do you relate more to Paul or Timothy in this passage? Why?

3. What problems in the church of Ephesus was Paul addressing in 1 Timothy? What was the root cause of these problems?

4. What is the goal of God's command of love? What are the characteristics of this love (vv. 4–5)?

5. According to verses 8–11 who is the Law intended for?

   ○ It is for people who are basically good.
   ○ It is for lawbreakers.
   ○ It is for people who are thinking about doing something wrong.
   ○ Other _____.

6. When did you first become aware of your sinfulness and your need for God? Has God been more of a "lawgiver" or a "lover" in your experience?

7. As you think about the characteristics of love found in verses 4–5, which one do you believe God desires for you to develop in your life?

Going Deeper   If your group has time and/or wants a challenge, go on to this question.

---

8. What are some controversies in the church today that may have been started by false teachers? How can we keep ourselves from being deceived?

 Caring Time Apply the Lesson and Pray for One Another (15 minutes)

The time spent praying for one another in the group is important for developing and expressing your concern for each other.

1. Agree on the group covenant and ground rules that are described in the introduction to this book.

2. Recall the group members' responses to question 7. How can the group pray for you today?

3. Share any other prayer requests and praises, and then close in prayer. Pray specifically for God to lead you to someone to bring next week to fill the empty chair.

Leader
Take some extra time in this first session to go over the introductory material at the beginning of this book. At the close, pass around your books and have everyone sign the Group Directory, also found in the front of this book.

NEXT WEEK *Today we considered the turmoil that is caused when false doctrine is taught in the church. We saw how Paul charged Timothy to restore the church to its original purpose of love. In the coming week, take some extra time with Jesus. Read 1 Timothy 1:1–11 again and ask Jesus to help you live your life with love that comes from a pure heart, a good conscience and a sincere faith. Next week we will look at how Paul encourages Timothy to challenge the false teaching that is disrupting the unity of the Ephesian church.*

Notes on 1 Timothy 1:1–11

Summary: Paul begins his letter by defining the nature of the problem in Ephesus. Certain elders, supposing themselves to be "teachers of the law" (v. 7), are in fact promoting "other doctrine" (v. 3) with the result that the church is in turmoil. Timothy's job (as Paul's representative) is to "command" (v. 3) them to stop doing this and restore the church to its original purpose, which is love (v. 5). The rest of the letter is an exposition of these basic themes.

1:1 *Paul, an apostle.* Paul uses the designation "an apostle" in his greeting, because his authority is in question or because he has an "official" word for the recipients of the letter. The presence of his title "apostle" here is an indication that although this letter is addressed to a friend (Timothy), it really is an official communication designed for the whole church. *according to the command of God.* The Greek word used here signifies a royal command that comes from a king or a god. It was God himself who gave him this role. Therefore, he speaks by the authority of God. *God our Savior.* It is normal for Paul in his greetings to add a title to the name of God (Phil. 1:2), but here and in Titus are the only two times Paul calls God "Savior." This was a title used for God in the Old Testament. It was also a term used by the mystery religions. Interestingly, Nero (who was emperor when Paul wrote) called himself the "Savior" of the world. So when Paul writes to Ephesus (a city where emperor worship was strong), he points out that God is the true source of salvation. *Jesus, our hope.* If God is the source of salvation, then Jesus is the one whom Christians trust to consummate that salvation upon his return.

1:2 *Grace, mercy, and peace.* The traditional Greek word at this point in a letter was *chairein* ("greetings"). In his earlier letters Paul had transformed this into a related but more Christian word (*charis* which means "grace") and then added the traditional Hebrew greeting *shalom* ("peace"). Only in the Pastoral Epistles does he add a third word to his blessing: "mercy," which further defines the impact of the Gospel on human life. The Gospel brings "grace, mercy and peace"—which is what Paul wishes for the church in Ephesus.

1:3 At this point in a letter, it was normal for Paul to offer a word of thanksgiving, but instead he goes right to the issue at hand—the false teachers. (Galatians, which also deals with false teaching, lacks a thanksgiving as well.) *remain in Ephesus.* Paul has had to go on to Macedonia, leaving Timothy behind in Ephesus. As he indicates in 3:14, the purpose of this letter is to instruct Timothy as to his role while there, in case he is delayed in returning to Ephesus (which Paul was, according to 2 Timothy). Paul's first instructions are found here in verse 3 ("remain in" and "command certain people"). ***Ephesus.*** The capital of the Roman Province of Asia, Ephesus was a large, bustling, secular city situated on the West coast of Asia Minor (modern Turkey) on the Aegean Sea. ***certain people.*** Who these false teachers are is not made clear in the letter. However, the evidence seems to indicate that they were elders from the Ephesian church itself. Paul warned in his farewell address to the Ephesian elders that "even from your own number men will arise and distort the truth in order to draw away disciples after them. So be on your guard!" (Acts 20:30–31a).

1:4 ***myths and endless genealogies.*** It is not easy to identify the exact nature of this teaching. The "myths" were probably connected both to Jewish speculation (such as in the Book of Jubilees) and to the legends that abounded in the ancient world, as were the genealogies. The Jews (in particular) were fascinated by genealogies. Some Jewish scholars took the family trees in the Old Testament and devoted great energy to constructing "biographies" for each character. These "biographies" were, of course, largely imaginary (i.e., "myths"). ***These promote empty speculations.*** All this speculation generated strife within the body, not "God's work." ***God's plan.*** God's plan for the redemption of the world, which stands in contrast to the "myths and genealogies."

1:5 The aim is to replace the quarrels and strife resulting from the controversy (6:3) with a new spirit of love. ***a pure heart.*** Jesus commends a pure heart in the sixth beatitude (Matt. 5:8), as does the Old Testament (Ps. 24:4; 51:10). In Scripture, the heart was considered to be the center of a person's being. If that center is not pure, love cannot radiate. ***a good conscience.*** Love cannot flow if the foundation of a person's moral consciousness is filled with shame (4:2). ***a sincere faith.*** Faith that is not genuine (as was the case with the "faith" of the false teachers) cannot issue in love.

1:6 ***fruitless discussion.*** The false teachers have turned away from these three Christian virtues, and are concerned instead meaningless talk.

1:7 ***teachers of the law.*** It is an honorable thing to be a "teacher of the law" (Acts 5:34) when the Law is understood properly. Apparently they were caught up in speculation about myths and genealogies found in Jewish writings.

1:8 ***the law is good.*** The Law accurately reflects God's will.

1:10 ***sexually immoral and homosexuals.*** Rabbis interpreted the seventh commandment to include all forms of sexual sin. ***kidnappers.*** The eighth commandment forbids stealing, which was interpreted to include stealing human beings. ***sound teaching.*** Literally, "wholesome teaching."

1:11 ***the glorious gospel.*** This is the source of sound doctrine.

Grace to Paul

Scripture 1 Timothy 1:12–20

> **LAST WEEK** *In last week's session, we studied Paul's command to Timothy to correct the false teachings that were spreading in the church at Ephesus. We were reminded that sound doctrine always has its basis in love, and that love results in having "a pure heart, a good conscience, and a sincere faith" (1:5). This week we will consider how the power of the Gospel can change the life of anyone, and how the person who has accepted Christ can then pass this life-changing experience on to others.*

 Ice-Breaker Connect With Your Group (15 minutes)

Leader
Begin the session with a word of prayer. Have your group members take turns sharing their responses to one, two or all three of the Ice-Breaker questions. Be sure that everyone gets a chance to participate.

There are many laws, rules and regulations that we must follow every day. We have probably all been caught in breaking some of these rules and then realizing our need for mercy. Paul was especially thankful for God's mercy, as he recalled how he had persecuted the church prior to his conversion. Take turns sharing your experiences with laws and mercy.

1. Which traffic law do you have the most difficulty obeying? Why?

   ○ The speed limit.
   ○ Stop signs.
   ○ Yielding to right-of-way traffic.
   ○ Signaling.
   ○ Wearing seat belts.
   ○ Other _____.

2. What rule did you have the hardest time with when you were a teenager?

   ○ Coming home by curfew.
   ○ Not being allowed to have certain friends.
   ○ Doing chores.
   ○ Not being allowed to wear the clothes or a particular hairstyle I wanted.
   ○ Other _____.

3. When you were growing up, who was responsible for punishing you when you broke the rules? Who showed mercy to you?

 # Bible Study Read Scripture and Discuss (30 minutes)

Paul gives us his personal testimony today, as he gives thanks and praise for God's grace in his life. He truly makes us feel hopeful that if God can change him, God can change anyone. With these words he encourages Timothy to persevere and "strongly engage in battle" (v. 18). Read 1 Timothy 1:12–20 and note how Paul expresses his thanks.

Leader
Ask three members of the group, selected ahead of time, to read aloud the Scripture passage. Have one person read verses 12–14; another read verses 15–17; and the third person read verses 18–20. Then discuss the Questions for Interaction, dividing into subgroups of three to six.

The Lord's Grace to Paul

Reader One: [12]I give thanks to Christ Jesus our Lord, who has strengthened me, because He considered me faithful, appointing me to the ministry— [13]one who was formerly a blasphemer, a persecutor, and an arrogant man. Since it was out of ignorance that I had acted in unbelief, I received mercy, [14]and the grace of our Lord overflowed, along with the faith and love that are in Christ Jesus.

Reader Two: [15]This saying is trustworthy and deserving of full acceptance: "Christ Jesus came into the world to save sinners"—and I am the worst of them. [16]But I received mercy because of this, so that in me, the worst of them, Christ Jesus might demonstrate the utmost patience as an example to those who would believe in Him for eternal life. [17]Now to the King eternal, immortal, invisible, the only God, be honor and glory forever and ever. Amen.

Reader Three: [18]Timothy, my child, I am giving you this instruction in keeping with the prophecies previously made about you, so that by them you may strongly engage in battle, [19]having faith and a good conscience. Some have rejected these and have suffered the shipwreck of their faith. [20]Hymenaeus and Alexander are among them, and I have delivered them to Satan, so that they may be taught not to blaspheme.

1 Timothy 1:12–20

Questions for Interaction

1. How would people describe your life before you met Jesus?

  ○ Fast and furious.
  ○ Party time.
  ○ One big mess.
  ○ Can't touch this.
  ○ Rowdy.
  ○ Wild and crazy.
  ○ Fairly routine.
  ○ One big brawl.
  ○ Other _____.

Leader
Refer to the Summary and Study Notes at the end of this session as needed. If 30 minutes is not enough time to answer all of the questions in this section, conclude the Bible Study by answering questions 6 and 7.

2. Before you met Jesus, in what ways did you deny Christ and encourage others to turn away from him (v. 13)?

3. What was Paul's life like before he had a personal encounter with Jesus?

4. In what ways does Paul's story give you hope or assurance?

5. Why is someone like Paul such a good witness to unbelievers (v. 16)?

6. In what ways can your story communicate God's mercy to others? When you share your past mistakes, what does that do?

7. In what area of your life do you need the mercy of Christ right now?

Going Deeper   If your group has time and/or wants a challenge, go on to this question.

8. What do you think it means that Paul delivered to Satan those who had "suffered the shipwreck of their faith" (vv. 19–20)? What did he hope this would accomplish?

Caring Time
Apply the Lesson and Pray for One Another (15 minutes)

Leader
Bring the group members back together and begin the Caring Time by sharing responses to all three questions. Then take turns giving prayer requests and having a time of group prayer.

Encourage and support one another in a time of sharing and prayer. Remember God's amazing mercy and his willingness to forgive.

1. If you were to describe this past week of your life in weather terms, what was it like?

   ○ Sunny and warm.
   ○ Partly cloudy with a chance for rain.
   ○ Cold and snowy.
   ○ Scattered showers.
   ○ Overcast and rainy.
   ○ Windblown.
   ○ Other _____

2. What is the forecast for next week? How can the group pray for you this coming week?

3. Who in your life needs you to give them mercy? What will you do this week to show them mercy and patience?

   P.S. *Add new group members to the Group Directory at the front of this book.*

NEXT WEEK *Today we witnessed the power of God's mercy in the life of the apostle Paul and how it so radically changed his life. His example shows us that no matter what we do, Jesus' sacrifice on the cross can change the hardest heart. In the coming week, read verses 12–20 again and meditate on the significance of Jesus' mercy in your life. Ask Jesus to help you to be merciful to others in the same way he has shown you mercy. Next week we will focus on some guidelines for worshiping God.*

Summary: One parenthetical statement leads to another. Having digressed in verses 8–11 to comment on the purpose of the Law (which the "teachers of the Law" had missed), Paul digresses a second time here to give his personal testimony (of the power of the Gospel to change sinners and make them into fit vehicles of the Gospel). Paul uses "I" and "me" some 14 times in this section. Perhaps this is a gentle encouragement to Timothy not to despair in confronting the false teachers. If Paul can be transformed, so can they.

1:12 *I give thanks to Christ Jesus.* Paul's response to being entrusted with the Gospel is one of thankfulness to Christ. Specifically, he is thankful for three things: for being empowered for the work, for being considered worthy for the job, and for actually being appointed to the task. *strengthened.* The reference is not to some sort of inward power but to the fact that Christ "made me equal to the task," as the NEB translates this word.

1:13 Paul is utterly amazed that he of all people was chosen for this high calling, given his past record. *blasphemer.* Paul had denied Christ and tried to force others to do the same (Acts 26:11). *a persecutor, and an arrogant man.* He had actively opposed the church—searching out Christians, arresting them, throwing them in prison, even voting for their deaths. *out of ignorance ... in unbelief.* Paul is not saying that he had received mercy because he was without guilt. All he is saying is that he acted "unintentionally" instead of "defiantly," using a common Old Testament distinction (Num. 15:22–31, compare Luke 23:34).

1:14 *faith and love that are in Christ Jesus.* God's grace brought "faith" where there had been "unbelief," and "love" where there had been "violence."

1:15 *This saying is trustworthy.* Paul uses this solemn formula four times in the Pastoral Epistles, but nowhere else in his writings (3:1; 4:9; 2 Tim. 2:11; Titus 3:8). Each time he follows it with what appears to be a quote (probably drawn from instructional material for new converts, from a creed or from some early liturgy). *Christ Jesus came into the world to save sinners.* With this quotation, Paul explains his own transformation (and also gives Timothy hope for the transformation of the false teachers). The emphasis here is on the Incarnation ("Jesus came into the world") and redemption ("to save sinners"). *I am the worst.* The mention of sinners reminds Paul of his own state. When he met Christ on the Damascus Road, he was overwhelmed both by the magnitude of his sin and by the expansiveness of God's grace. *I am.* Paul uses the present tense, not the past tense ("I was"). He is still a sinner; that is, he is flawed and fallen. However, he has been forgiven and redeemed, and so he presses on to serve the Savior who brought about this new reality.

1:16 *I received mercy.* Paul picks up the phrase he used in verse 13 and then describes the reason for God's gracious intervention in his life. *an example.* Paul is an illustration (or demonstration) of what can happen to anyone. *believe in Him.* Conversion occurs when individuals accept Jesus by faith and place their trust in him. *eternal life.* People receive the gift of eternal life when they place their trust in Christ. The Greek phrase translated "eternal life" means not so much "life without end" (though it implies that) as it does the "life of the coming age." Those who are in Christ can experience this life in the here-and-now, but it will only be fully known when Christ returns again.

1:17 *the King eternal.* This title is suggested by the idea of "eternal life" in the previous verse. It is a phrase drawn from Jewish sources. *Amen.* This is also a Jewish phrase that was used in the synagogues to signify agreement with the prayers that had been pronounced.

1:18 *I am giving you this instruction.* The word for "giving" means to entrust something valuable into the safekeeping of someone else. *the prophecies previously made about you.* Perhaps Paul is referring to the prophecies at the time of Timothy's ordination (4:14). (The commissioning of Barnabas and Saul in Acts 13:1–3 also involved prophecy.) *engage in battle.* It will be tough for Timothy in Ephesus as he comes up against the leadership of the church. Using a war metaphor, Paul encourages him to remember his divine call when the going gets rough, and so be encouraged to carry on the battle.

1:19 *faith and a good conscience.* Once again, as in verse 5, Paul links faith and conscience. Paul urges Timothy to hold on to these (in contrast to those who have intentionally repudiated their faith and conscience). By not listening to their consciences, they have "shipwrecked their faith."

1:20 *Hymenaeus and Alexander.* Apparently, these are two of the erring teachers in Ephesus. Hymenaeus is mentioned again in 2 Timothy 2:17 (along with Philetus) as one who taught that the resurrection was already past. An Alexander (a metalworker) is also mentioned in 2 Timothy 4:14–15 as having harmed Paul grievously. This may be the same Alexander that is mentioned here, although there is yet another Alexander in Ephesus. This is the Alexander who tried to speak at the time of the riot against Paul (Acts 19:33). Since the name Alexander is quite common it is not clear if these are all the same person or different people. *delivered them to Satan.* Paul excluded them from the church; i.e., they were expelled from the Christian fellowship and sent back into the world (which is Satan's realm—1 Cor. 5:5). *may be taught not to blaspheme.* The hope was that they might be restored to faith by this form of discipline. It is not by accident that Paul mentions that he too was once a "blasphemer" (v. 13), but by the grace of God he came to faith (v. 14).

Instructions on Worship and Prayer

Scripture 1 Timothy 2:1–15

> **LAST WEEK** *Paul's testimony to God's grace in his life was our topic in last week's session. We were reminded that no matter what we do, God can and will forgive us because of the sacrifice that Jesus made on the cross. This week we will focus our attention on the guidelines Paul gives to the Ephesian church concerning worship and prayer.*

 Ice-Breaker Connect With Your Group (15 minutes)

Leader
Choose one or two Ice-Breaker questions. If you have a new group member you may want to do all three. Remember to stick closely to the three-part agenda and the time allowed for each segment.

The way we look is important to many of us. The types and styles of clothes we wear can say a great deal about our personality and even reflect our beliefs. Paul realized the importance of how we appear as part of our Christian witness, and he addressed the issue in today's Scripture reading. Take turns sharing your thoughts and experiences with your appearance.

1. In high school, what were your favorite clothes to wear? What were you not allowed to wear?

	Couldn't wear	Loved to wear
Clothes that were too tight.	_____	_____
Clothes that were too loose.	_____	_____
Skirts that were too short.	_____	_____
Favorite running shoes.	_____	_____
Dressed like my favorite singing group.	_____	_____
Clothes that showed too much.	_____	_____
Clothes that were too nice.	_____	_____

2. What kind of clothes shopper are you?

- ○ Hit and run.
- ○ I can shop for hours.
- ○ I avoid shopping as much as possible.
- ○ I love finding bargains at garage sales.
- ○ Other _____.

3. What do you usually wear when you go to church?

- ○ My best.
- ○ What I'm expected to wear.
- ○ What makes me feel comfortable.
- ○ What makes me look good.
- ○ Whatever I feel like.
- ○ Other _____.

Bible Study Read Scripture and Discuss (30 minutes)

In today's passage, Paul gives some very specific guidelines on how the Ephesians should behave when they worship and pray. He wants them to realize that they should no longer live according to the culture around them, so that God will be glorified in all they do. Read 1 Timothy 2:1–15 and note the reasons that Paul gives for each of his instructions.

Leader

Select a member of the group ahead of time to read aloud the Scripture passage. Then discuss the Questions for Interaction, dividing into subgroups of three to six. Be sure each subgroup member is getting a chance to participate in the discussion.

Instructions on Worship and Prayer

2 First of all, then, I urge that petitions, prayers, intercessions, and thanksgivings be made for everyone, [2]for kings and all those who are in authority, so that we may lead a tranquil and quiet life in all godliness and dignity. [3]This is good, and it pleases God our Savior, [4]who wants everyone to be saved and to come to the knowledge of the truth.
[5]For there is one God
and one mediator between God and man,
a man, Christ Jesus,
[6]who gave Himself—a ransom for all,
a testimony at the proper time.
[7]For this I was appointed a herald, an apostle (I am telling the truth; I am not lying), and a teacher of the Gentiles in faith and truth.
[8]Therefore I want the men in every place to pray, lifting up holy hands without anger or argument. [9]Also, the women are to dress themselves in modest clothing, with decency and good sense; not with elaborate hairstyles, gold, pearls, or expensive apparel, [10]but with good works, as is proper

for women who affirm that they worship God. [11]A woman should learn in silence with full submission. [12]I do not allow a woman to teach or to have authority over a man; instead, she is to be silent. [13]For Adam was created first, then Eve. [14]And Adam was not deceived, but the woman was deceived and transgressed. [15]But she will be saved through childbearing, if she continues in faith, love, and holiness, with good sense.

1 Timothy 2:1–15

Questions for Interaction

Leader
Refer to the Summary and Study Notes at the end of this session as needed. If 30 minutes is not enough time to answer all of the questions in this section, conclude the Bible Study by answering question 7.

1. What policies or guidelines does your church have for worship? How do the instructions for worship in this passage compare with them?

2. What do you enjoy the most when you pray to God?

   ○ Thanking him for all he has done.
   ○ Praising him for who he is.
   ○ Escaping from the routine of life.
   ○ Telling him what's happening in my life.
   ○ Just being in his presence.
   ○ Asking him to bless my friends.
   ○ Other _____.

3. What do you think the false teachers are teaching about prayer that causes Paul to write verses 3–7?

   ○ Style points count with God.
   ○ The louder the better.
   ○ It's the time to deliver a sermon.
   ○ It's time to say things you couldn't other wise.
   ○ It is for the people around you.
   ○ More is better.
   ○ You must seem to be pious.
   ○ Pray only for the saints.
   ○ Pray only for those you agree with.
   ○ Other _____.

4. What can hinder or hurt us from worshiping God together (v. 8)? What can help?

5. What do you think Paul means when he uses the phrase, "is to be silent" (see notes on verse 12)?

6. Regardless of how verses 11–15 are interpreted, the ministry of women has been controversial. What is the best way to understand this passage and still allow women to use their gifts and make a meaningful contribution to the body of Christ.

7. What can you do to honor God in the next worship service you participate in? How can you help others worship him?

Going Deeper   If your group has time and/or wants a challenge, go on to this question.

8. In verse 11, Paul talks about submission. What kind of submission are we all to have (1 Peter 2:13–21; 3:1–7)?

 Caring Time Apply the Lesson and Pray for One Another (15 minutes)

Prayer and worship are important and vital for Christian community. As you begin this Caring Time, enter with an attitude of "faith, love, and holiness," as Paul described in the passage we read today.

1. One of Paul's points this week is that we should pray for everyone, believer and unbeliever alike. Who is it that God desires you to pray for today? How can the group specifically pray for that person?

2. Who do you know that needs to be part of your loving community (to fill our empty chair)?

3. What is your biggest concern about the coming week? (After each person answers the question, take time to pray for him or her before going to the next group member.)

Leader
To begin the Caring Time you may want to consider singing a song of worship that the group would be familiar with to enter into an attitude of prayer. When the group prays for the empty chair have the group members put their hands on the chair as the group prays.

NEXT WEEK *Today we were challenged by instructions for prayer and worship that Paul gave to the Ephesian church. He was calling them back to the way they conducted themselves before the false teachers gained influence. In the coming week, follow through on your answer to question 7 and make your worship more meaningful in some way. Next week we will read and study the qualifications Paul gives to Timothy for leaders of the church. These qualifications will give Timothy a baseline for disciplining these erring leaders.*

Summary: Having completed his twofold charge to Timothy (1:3,18), Paul now moves on to three sets of specific instructions concerning: (1) the proper subjects for prayer (vv. 1–7), (2) the proper demeanor for prayer and worship (vv. 8–15), and (3) the qualifications for leadership in the church.

2:1 *First of all.* This conjunction (which could also be translated "therefore") links the preceding problem of false teachers with the forthcoming instructions about prayer and worship. This is important to note since chapters 2 and 3 have often been considered a "church manual of conduct and order" with little or no relationship to the problem of false teachers. Understanding that these instructions are to be directed at the problem of the erring teachers. Paul is not saying to a church without structure: "This is how you do it." These activities were already present. Paul is seeking to restore these practices to the uncorrupted form they had prior to the influence of the false teachers. ***petitions, prayers, intercessions, and thanksgivings.*** Although Paul uses four words for prayer, it is not possible to distinguish sharply between them. His point is that all types of prayer should be made for all people. ***everyone.*** This is where Paul's emphasis is placed in this verse (and paragraph). No one, be they secular ruler (v. 2) or pagan unbeliever (v. 4), should be left out of their prayers.

2:2 *that we may lead a tranquil and quiet life.* This is the reason why prayer should be offered for those in authority.

2:4 *who wants everyone to be saved.* Salvation is necessary to escape divine wrath on the Day of Judgment. ***to come to the knowledge of the truth.*** This is necessary in order to be saved. "Knowledge" carries with it the idea not only of "understanding" the truth but "accepting" it by faith and thus building a life on the basis of that truth. Paul emphasizes knowing the truth in contrast to the false truth of the erring teachers.

2:5 *there is one God.* Because there is only one God, there is no other god to whom people can appeal for salvation. ***one mediator.*** A mediator is an individual who brings two estranged parties together. In contrast to Judaism, which asserted that Moses and the angels (Gal. 3:19–20) were mediators between God and the people, Paul asserts that Jesus is the unique mediator who acts as a go-between, reconciling fallen humanity with the one God. ***a man, Christ Jesus.*** He is able to be this because he is himself a human being. (The term here for "man" is the generic word, not the Greek word for male gender.)

2:6 *a ransom for all.* Paul's emphasis is not so much on the means by which Jesus became the mediator ("ransom"), but the fact that his sacrifice was for "all," i.e., universal in scope.

2:8 Paul moves to the question of the proper demeanor for prayer. His first point is that when Christians come together, they ought to do so to pray, not to argue. ***lifting up holy hands.*** Paul's emphasis is on "holy" hands (those that have not been soiled by controversy).

2:12 *I do not allow.* By this phrase Paul focuses on the specific situation in Ephesus. He obviously does not feel that women cannot engage in ministry, as evidenced by his statements in places like Romans 16:1–3 and Philippians 4:2–3. But in Ephesus (given the turmoil caused by the false teachers and the complicity of certain women in this heresy), Paul's instructions are for them to back off and assume a quieter role. ***to teach or to have authority.*** The crucial issue here is whether Paul is giving two separate prohibitions (women are not to teach and are not to have authority over men), or if he is joining together two parts of a related prohibition (women are not to teach men with authority). The question revolves around his use of the conjunction *oude* ("or"). Every other place that Paul uses *oude* in this sort of construction, he appears to be presenting a single, coherent idea or related concepts. So it seems likely that what he is prohibiting here is women teaching in a position of authority. *authority.* Paul uses an unusual word here. (This is its only occurrence in the New Testament.) It often carries the sense of "domineering" or "acting on one's own authority"—which is the root meaning of the verb. If Paul had been concerned with the usual exercise of authority, he would most likely have used a more familiar word. *she is to be silent.* The instructions in verses 11–12 begin and end with an appeal for women to learn from the Word of God.

2:15 This has been a notoriously difficult verse to translate and even more difficult to interpret. As the church fathers understood it, this probably refers to the child borne by woman—that "Seed" who would overcome Satan and the effects of the Fall (Gen. 3:15)—namely Christ and the woman, Mary. It may refer to the unique task that women have in bearing children. It is most likely focusing on the grace that comes as humility and self-control to the a woman who recognizes her unique value in God's plan.

Leadership in the Church

Scripture 1 Timothy 3:1–16

LAST WEEK *In last week's session, we were challenged by Paul's instructions for prayer and worship. This week we will look at qualities that church leaders should possess. We will see how Paul uses these instructions to help Timothy deal with leaders of the Ephesian church who have chosen to distort sound biblical teaching.*

Ice-Breaker Connect With Your Group (15 minutes)

Leader
Use all three Ice-Breakers to help a new person in the group feel welcome and get to know others in the group. Remember to stick closely to the three-part agenda and the time allowed for each segment.

Those who are in leadership positions can exert a great amount of influence on those who look up to them. This is especially true for the spiritual leaders in the church. Take turns sharing your thoughts about and experiences with leadership.

1. What well-known leader in the recent history of the church do you especially admire?

2. What would you most want to accomplish if you were president of the United States?

   ○ Reform health care.
   ○ Work on the moral framework of the country.
   ○ Develop policies for economic growth.
   ○ Help people get jobs.
   ○ Combat terrorism.
   ○ Other _____.

3. If you were elected as the mayor of the city, what is the first policy you would enact?

Bible Study Read Scripture and Discuss (30 minutes)

Leader
Ask three members of the group, selected ahead of time, to read aloud the Scripture passage. Have the first person read 3:1–7; the second person read 3:8–13; and the third person read 3:14–16. Then subdivide into subgroups of three to six and discuss the Questions for Interaction.

Now that Paul has given instructions on the proper way to pray and worship, he goes on to tell Timothy the qualifications he should require in the overseers and deacons of the church. In this way, Paul and Timothy can be assured that sound teaching and leadership will prevail, and the false teachers will be disciplined. Read 1 Timothy 3:1–16 and note how the entire family of each leader is included in these qualifications.

Leadership in the Church

Reader One: 3 This saying is trustworthy: "If anyone aspires to be an overseer, he desires a noble work." [2]An overseer, therefore, must be above reproach, the husband of one wife, self-controlled, sensible, respectable, hospitable, an able teacher, [3]not addicted to wine, not a bully but gentle, not quarrelsome, not greedy— [4]one who manages his own household competently, having his children under control with all dignity. [5](If anyone does not know how to manage his own household, how will he take care of God's church?) [6]He must not be a new convert, or he might become conceited and fall into the condemnation of the Devil. [7]Furthermore, he must have a good reputation among outsiders, so that he does not fall into disgrace and the Devil's trap.

Reader Two: [8]Deacons, likewise, should be worthy of respect, not hypocritical, not drinking a lot of wine, not greedy for money, [9]holding the mystery of the faith with a clear conscience. [10]And they must also be tested first; if they prove blameless, then they can serve as deacons. [11]Wives, too, must be worthy of respect, not slanderers, self-controlled, faithful in everything. [12]Deacons must be husbands of one wife, managing their children and their own households competently. [13]For those who have served well as deacons acquire a good standing for themselves, and great boldness in the faith that is in Christ Jesus.

Reader Three: [14]I write these things to you, hoping to come to you soon. [15]But if I should be delayed, I have written so that you will know how people ought to act in God's household, which is the church of the living God, the pillar and foundation of the truth. And most certainly, the mystery of godliness is great:
[16]He was manifested in the flesh,
justified in the Spirit,
seen by angels,
preached among the Gentiles,
believed on in the world,
taken up in glory.

1 Timothy 3:1–16

Questions for Interaction

Leader
Refer to the Summary and Study Notes at the conclusion of this session as needed. If 30 minutes is not enough time to answer all of the questions in this section, conclude the Bible Study by answering question 7.

1. What are the top three qualities you look for in a pastor? Which one of these three qualities is most important to you?

2. What is the best quality of your pastor(s)?

   ○ Dignified.
   ○ Friendly and warm.
   ○ Able to teach.
   ○ Good sense of humor
   ○ Truthful and honest.
   ○ Great dresser.
   ○ Caring and kind.
   ○ Gentle.
   ○ Other _____.

3. What is Paul's main concern in giving Timothy these qualifications for leadership?

4. What do you believe will happen if they apply these standards to the leaders in the Ephesian church? How would your church be different using these standards?

5. What does it mean for a church leader to have a "good reputation among outsiders" (v. 7)? Why is this important?

6. What central facts about Jesus are summed up in the hymn (v. 16)? How have people or society tried to convince you that these beliefs couldn't possibly be true?

7. What leadership roles do you have in your life? Which quality listed here are you strongest in? Which one are you weakest in? How would you like God to help you develop your weakest trait?

Going Deeper   If your group has time and/or wants a challenge, go on to this question.

8. What is the principle in verses 4–5 and 12? What if a godly man who meets the other qualifications has a child who is rebellious and a troublemaker?

Caring Time Apply the Lesson and Pray for One Another (15 minutes)

Take time to share how God is working in your life and to encourage and support one another. Pray for each other's concerns and needs and remember to include prayer for the empty chair.

Leader
Begin the Caring Time by sharing responses to all three of the questions in this section. Plan accordingly so that every member has adequate time to participate and answer each question.

1. How would you describe your relationship with God today?

   ○ Close.
   ○ Distant.
   ○ Improving.
   ○ Strained.
   ○ God who?
   ○ Other _____.

2. How would you like the group to pray for you regarding your answer to question 7?

3. In the course of next week, what can you or your group do to support and help your church leaders?

NEXT WEEK *Our study today revolved around the qualifications for church leaders. We were reminded how important it is for all Christians to conduct their lives in a way that honors God and his kingdom. Take some time this week and reflect on what your life says to others about God. Next week we will be challenged to understand and deal with evil and chaos in the church. We will look at specific ways we can lead by example to change the hearts and minds of those who have been deceived by Satan.*

Summary: Paul communicates his third set of instructions here in chapter 3. These instructions are the qualifications for leadership in the church. In this passage he discusses two types of leaders: "overseers" (vv. 1–7) and "deacons" (vv. 8–13). This list of qualifications is given not only to assist Timothy in finding the right leaders, but also to help him deal with the false teachers already in place. By establishing standards for leadership, Paul gives Timothy the basis on which to discipline those teachers who are behaving in undesirable ways. The problem is not with the performance of duties but with a deviance in lifestyle and teaching. Notice that these qualifications are all outward in orientation. They deal with what others can observe. Furthermore, none of these qualifications is distinctly Christian. They reflect what first-century culture considered the highest ideals. Paul continues to be concerned that the church not be disgraced before the world (v. 7).

3:1 *This saying is trustworthy.* This is the second time Paul uses this phrase (1:15) and again he is probably quoting a saying they already know and accept. *overseer.* Sometimes translated "bishop," this title probably did not mean in the first century what "bishop" has come to mean today (the chief episcopal officer presiding over many churches). This is the word used for the office of elder. *a noble work.* Paul's point is that the position of overseer is a high calling (despite the abuse of the office by some).

3:2 *above reproach.* Paul begins with an all-encompassing category: there should be no obvious defect in the character of the overseer that would cause people to question the appointment. *husband of one wife.* Literally, "a one-woman man." Paul could mean four things by this. First, that church leaders must be married, in contrast to the false teachers who were forbidding marriage. (However, this is unlikely since Paul and Timothy were probably not married.) Second, that polygamy was forbidden. Third, that second marriages were forbidden whether due to divorce or death of one's spouse. (Yet, he says in 5:14 what amounts almost to a "command" to young widows to remarry.) Fourth, the most likely meaning is that sexual faithfulness to one's spouse was demanded; that is, the married life of the overseer must be exemplary—in contrast

to the widespread infidelity of that day. *self-controlled / respectable.* These companion terms were considered in Greek literature to be great virtues. The first word, *sophron,* has been variously rendered as "prudent," "of sound mind," and "chaste." The second word, *kosmios,* can be translated "well-behaved," "orderly," or "dignified," and refers to the person who is a good citizen. In other words, if a person is self-controlled in their outer conduct, it is because they are respectable in their inner life. *hospitable.* Overseers must be willing to open up their homes to guests. It was a common practice in the first century to offer hospitality to travelers since the inns were notorious for their dirt and immorality, not to mention their expense (5:10; Rom. 12:13; 1 Peter 4:9). *an able teacher.* This is the one quality that implies a function. Paul will say more about this in 5:17.

3:3 *not addicted to wine.* Paul is not forbidding the drinking of wine (which was widely used in his time, due to poor water supplies), only overindulgence. Drunkenness was a serious problem in the first century. *not a bully but gentle.* "Not a bully" means literally "not a giver of blows"; "gentle" refers to those who do not seek to apply the letter of the law in cases where to do so would bring injustice.

3:5 *manage.* This word contains the idea of guidance and active caregiving—in the home and in the church.

3:6 *new convert.* Literally, "newly planted." The temptation in a new church is to put into office people of standing and influence who have been recently converted. Paul describes the danger in doing this. *conceited.* Literally, "to be filled with smoke." It was said that the false teachers were conceited (6:4). Perhaps some of them were recent converts.

3:8 *Deacons.* Paul often describes himself and others as a *diakonos* ("deacon"), a word variously translated as "servant" or "minister." The root idea of the word is that of doing menial tasks, such as serving at tables (Luke 17:8; 22:26; John 12:2). The order of deacons has traditionally been associated with the seven men listed in Acts 6 but, in fact, they are never called "deacons" and they did teach. *worthy of respect.* Once again Paul begins with an all-encompassing term to describe the character of these office holders. They are to be "serious" and "to have a good character." *not hypocritical, not drinking a lot of wine, not greedy for money.* Paul follows this with three prohibitions. They are to be "straight," literally, "not double-tongued." They must not think one thing and say another. Also,

like overseers, they must not be given to excess wine or be greedy.

3:10 *tested.* Paul does not explain the nature of this test. Perhaps it involves a probation period that included a formal exam. More likely, it involved the evaluation of their character prior to their appointment (1 Cor. 16:3; 2 Cor. 13:5).

3:11 It is not clear about whom Paul is writing here—the wives of the deacons or women who were deacons—since the word *gyne* can mean either "wife" or "woman." It is interesting to note the fact that the same four qualities listed in verse 8 are given here (in parallel form) in the same order, which may indicate that Paul is referring to women who hold this office.)

3:16 Paul ends by quoting a hymn from the early church. One way to interpret this hymn is to understand that the first stanza of three lines is focusing on the earthly ministry of Jesus. It begins with his incarnation ("manifested in the flesh"), and then moves to his resurrection ("justified in the Spirit") and his glorification ("seen by angels"). It is not clear why Paul includes this hymn here, but perhaps its "truth" (v. 15) stands in sharp contrast to the teaching of the false teachers (to whom he returns in chapter 4).

Dealing With Chaos

Scripture 1 Timothy 4:1–16

LAST WEEK *In last week's session, the qualifications for leadership in the church were outlined to give Timothy a basis for disciplining the false teachers. We were reminded how these qualifications can also be a guideline for how we conduct our lives as Christians. Today we will focus on how to minister during times of chaos caused by heresy in the church.*

Ice-Breaker Connect With Your Group (15 minutes)

Sometimes it's very hard to distinguish the truth from lies. People will say or do just about anything to get us to buy their product or believe the way they do. Take turns sharing your experiences with deception.

Leader
It is important to start each group time by connecting the members. Use one, two or all three of the Ice-Breaker questions to help get your group talking to each other.

1. As a child, what happened when you were caught in a lie?

   ○ Someone washed my mouth out with soap.
   ○ It was hard for me to sit down for a couple of days.
   ○ I usually was grounded.
   ○ I had to apologize.
   ○ Other _____.

2. What is the most deceptive commercial or print advertisement you have ever seen? What made it deceptive?

3. Have you ever been caught trying to deceive someone? What happened?

Bible Study Read Scripture and Discuss (30 minutes)

Paul continues to deal with the problem of the false teachers and what Timothy must do to minister in this situation. He doesn't just want Timothy to abandon these elders who have gone astray. Paul wants him to point out how their teachings are deceptive, hoping to bring them back to the truth. Read 1 Timothy 4:1–16 and note the importance of perseverance and commitment to our faith.

Dealing With Chaos

Reader One: 4 Now the Spirit explicitly says that in the latter times some will depart from the faith, paying attention to deceitful spirits and the teachings of demons, [2]through the hypocrisy of liars whose consciences are seared. [3]They forbid marriage and demand abstinence from foods that God created to be received with gratitude by those who believe and know the truth. [4]For everything created by God is good, and nothing should be rejected if it is received with thanksgiving, [5]since it is sanctified by the word of God and by prayer.

Reader Two: [6]If you point these things out to the brothers, you will be a good servant of Christ Jesus, nourished by the words of the faith and of the good teaching that you have followed. [7]But have nothing to do with irreverent and silly myths. Rather, train yourself in godliness, [8]for,

the training of the body has a limited benefit,
but godliness is beneficial in every way
since it holds promise for the present life
and also for the life to come.

Reader One: [9]This saying is trustworthy and deserves full acceptance. [10]In fact, we labor and strive for this, because we have put our hope in the living God, who is the Savior of everyone, especially of those who believe.
[11]Command and teach these things. [12]No one should despise your youth; instead, you should be an example to the believers in speech, in conduct, in love, in faith, in purity. [13]Until I come, give your attention to public reading, exhortation, and teaching. [14]Do not neglect the gift that is in you; it was given to you through prophecy, with the laying on of hands by the council of elders.

Reader Two: [15]Practice these things; be committed to them, so that your progress may be evident to all. [16]Be conscientious about yourself and your teaching; persevere in these things, for by doing this you will save both yourself and your hearers.

1 Timothy 4:1–16

Questions for Interaction

Leader
Refer to the Summary and Study Notes at the end of the session as needed. If you find that 30 minutes is not enough time to answer all of the questions in this section, conclude the Study by answering question 7.

1. If a person or group was teaching something I thought was unbiblical in my church, the first thing I would do is:

   ○ Change churches.
   ○ Deal with the problem head on.
   ○ Seek advice of trusted friends.
   ○ Confront only those I needed to confront.
   ○ Take it before the church.
   ○ Ignore the problem.
   ○ Other _____.

2. How does Paul describe those who are causing trouble and chaos in the church (vv. 1–3)?

3. What are these elders teaching that is false and hypocritical? How should Timothy address the situation?

4. How would you explain to someone what Paul means by "godliness" (v. 7; see also vv. 11–16)? How does this lifestyle differ from the self-denial taught by the false teachers (v. 3)?

5. What role does age play in being an influence in the lives of others (v. 12)? Has anyone ever put down what you have said about God because of your age? Describe what happened.

6. Do you spend more time and energy on physical training or training for godliness? Explain your answer.

7. What is one area of your life where you need to do more training for godliness? How can you make better use of your God-given gifts (v. 14)?

Going Deeper   If your group has time and/or wants a challenge, go on to this question.

1. Are there any limits to the freedom principle of verses 4–5? If so, what are they?

Caring Time
Apply the Lesson and Pray for One Another (15 minutes)

Leader
Caring Time is one of the most important parts of our group time. Ask God to reveal each person's needs and challenge group members to pray for and affirm each other during the coming week.

What has God been doing in your life? Take some time to reflect on these three questions. Answer them honestly, and then pray for each other sincerely.

1. In what area of your life do you believe God wants you to set an example for other believers this week (explain your answer)?

   ○ My speech.
   ○ My life.
   ○ My love.
   ○ My faith.
   ○ My purity.
   ○ Other _____.

2. In what situation do you need to put your "hope in the living God" (v. 10) in the coming week?

3. Pray for each other in regard to your answers to question 7. How can the group support you as you train for godliness and use your gifts?

NEXT WEEK *Today we saw that, no matter what our age, God wants us to address deception, false teaching and chaos in the church. We were reminded how we must live our life in devotion to God, desiring to grow in holiness love, faith and purity. In the coming week, evaluate your priorities and see how much time you are really giving to your spiritual training and development. Next week we will look at specific attitudes that we must have concerning our relationships to others.*

Summary: Paul returns to the subject of the false teachers and how Timothy can deal with them—topics he first introduced in chapter one. In verses 1–5, he comments on the false teachers and what they are teaching. Then in verses 6–16, he gives instructions to Timothy on how to minister in this situation.

4:1 *the Spirit explicitly says.* Paul does not identify the specific prophecy he has in mind. However, the idea that people will stray from God in the last days is found at other places in Scripture (Mark 13:22; 2 Tim. 3:1–5). *latter times.* Paul believed that they were living in the last days just prior to Christ's return, a time when there would be great evil (2 Thess. 2:3–12). *some.* Paul refers to those Christians in Ephesus who have fallen victim to the "liars" (v. 2) or the false teachers in the church. *deceitful spirits and ... demons.* This is the source of the false doctrine. Satan is behind the chaos in the Ephesian church as he has been in other churches (2 Cor. 2:11).

4:2 *hypocrisy of liars.* Not only is their doctrine demon-inspired, they themselves are, literally, "speakers of falsehood". Furthermore, they are hypocritical. Paul hints that they may not, in fact, be living what they are teaching. They may not be quite as ethical as they pretend to be (6:3–5). *consciences are seared.* Their moral judgment has been "cauterized" so that they are no longer able to distinguish between truth and falsehood. Alternatively, this phrase may mean that by accepting the lies of Satan, they have been branded with his mark as his servants. (Slaves were sometimes branded on their foreheads with their owner's sign.)

4:4 *everything created by God is good.* This is the teaching about God in which Paul teaches about the Christian's response to "forbidden" foods. *thanksgiving.* Paul is referring to the gratitude expressed to God by means of the "grace" that is said prior to a meal.

4:6 *point these things out.* Paul's gentle tone is evident right from the beginning. He does not say that Timothy must "order" or "command" the brothers and sisters in the church. What he is to do is more akin to "suggesting" than it is to "instructing." *servant.* The word Paul uses here is *diakonos*, which is translated "deacon" in 3:8.

4:7 Having told Timothy to hold on to what is true, Paul now warns him to avoid what is false. *silly myths.* In Greek literature it was used as a sarcastic reference to the sort of stories that were passed around while the superstitious old women sat talking. *train yourself in godliness.* In contrast to practicing strict self-denial as a measure of personal spiritual discipline (v. 3), Paul now proposes a genuinely Christian form of self-discipline.

4:8 *training of the body.* Having used an athletic image, Paul then comments on it in passing. While affirming the value of physical exercise, Paul's real interest is in spiritual exercise ("godliness"). *promise for the present life and also for the life to come.* The "life" Paul refers to is the "eternal life" one receives through belief in Jesus (1:16). It is this quality of life—in both the present and the future—that is promised to those who practice "godliness."

4:10 *we have put our hope.* Paul elaborates on why Christians pursue godliness with such vigor. It is because they have placed their hope in God who is alive and the one who brings salvation (new life) to all. The verb tense indicates a continuous state of hope and not just a single act. *especially of those who believe.* We see a difference between the general grace of God to all people and the gift of eternal life for those who believe in Christ.

4:11 *Command.* The first thing Paul says is that Timothy must speak with authority. The impression given here in verses 11–12 and elsewhere (1 Cor. 16:10–11; 2 Tim. 1:6–9) is that Timothy was a somewhat diffident, even timid, person. Timothy is in the middle of a hard situation in Ephesus, and Paul does not want him to be taken advantage of, so he encourages him to be more forceful. Since this was a public letter, Paul is declaring to all who will read it that Timothy has been empowered by him to "command and teach."

4:12 *youth.* The problem may have to do with Timothy's age. He is probably only in his early 30s. However, he is living in a culture that respected age. Furthermore, the teachers that he is called upon to discipline are almost surely older than he. *be an example.* There is little he can do about his age, but Timothy can lead by example. Paul identifies five areas in which he is to model Christian conduct. "Speech" and "conduct" refer to day-by-day conversation and behavior. "Love" (*agape*), "faith" (faithfulness), and "purity" (not only chastity but general integrity) refer to inner qualities that show themselves through an outer lifestyle. In contrast, the false teachers are contentious in speech and errant in behavior. They have abandoned love and faith and their purity is based on a non-Christian asceticism.

4:13 *public reading.* This is the first reference to the use of Scripture in Christian worship. What Timothy would be reading is, of course, the Old Testament. Public reading was something of an art, since the early manuscripts had no divisions between the words and minimal punctuation. *teaching.* This is instruction in Christian doctrine.

4:14 *laying on of hands.* Appointment to office (ordination) was accompanied by the laying on of hands (literally, the pressing of hands) by the commissioning body (here, the elders). This was modeled on the Jewish rite of ordination of rabbis, which in turn found its root in the ordination of Joshua (Num. 27:18–23; Deut. 34:9).

Specific Advice

Scripture 1 Timothy 5:1–6:2

LAST WEEK *Last week we considered how confusing things can become when the leaders in the church abandon what is true about God and his kingdom. In times like these we must encourage one another to grow in holiness, love, faith and purity. Today we will look at some specific advice that Paul gives to Timothy regarding relationships and responsibilities within the church.*

 Ice-Breaker Connect With Your Group (15 minutes)

There are times when we all need help. Some need help moving furniture, others need a ride to the airport and others face financial hardship. In these times people turn to the people around them. Take turns sharing your experiences with giving or needing help.

Leader
Choose one or two of the Ice-Breaker questions. If you have a new group member you might want to do all three to help them get acquainted. Remember to stick closely to the three-part agenda and the time allowed for each segment.

1. As you were growing up who was the older person that helped you with guidance in difficult times?

   ○ Grandparent.
   ○ Parent.
   ○ Teacher.
   ○ Pastor.
   ○ Sibling.
   ○ Neighbor.
   ○ Friend.
   ○ Other _____.

2. What kind of volunteer work have you done for your church or another organization that helps needy people?

3. If you were in a financial bind, who would you go to for help, and why?

- ○ Dad.
- ○ Mom.
- ○ Boss.
- ○ Grandparents.
- ○ Friend.
- ○ Brother or sister.
- ○ Other _____.

Bible Study Read Scripture and Discuss (30 minutes)

How we treat others is an important part of being a Christian. In this passage, Paul gives specific guidelines as to how Timothy and others in the church should relate to older and younger men and women, widows and slaves. Read 1 Timothy 5:1–6:2 and note how love is the basis for all of these commands.

Leader
Ask three group members, selected ahead of time, to read aloud the Scripture passage. Then discuss the Questions for Interaction, dividing into subgroups of three to six.

Specific Advice

Reader One: 5 Do not rebuke an older man, but exhort him as a father, younger men as brothers, [2]older women as mothers, and with all propriety, the younger women as sisters.

[3]Support widows who are genuinely widows. [4]But if any widow has children or grandchildren, they should learn to practice their religion toward their own family first and to repay their parents, for this pleases God. [5]The real widow, left all alone, has put her hope in God and continues night and day in her petitions and prayers; [6]however, she who is self-indulgent is dead even while she lives.

Reader Two: [7]Command this, so that they won't be blamed. [8]Now if anyone does not provide for his own relatives, and especially for his household, he has denied the faith and is worse than an unbeliever.

Reader Three: [9]No widow should be placed on the official support list unless she is at least 60 years old, has been the wife of one husband, [10]and is well known for good works—that is, if she has brought up children, shown hospitality, washed the saints' feet, helped the afflicted, and devoted herself to every good work. [11]But refuse to enroll younger widows; for when they are drawn away from Christ by desire, they want to marry, [12]and will therefore receive condemnation because they have renounced their original pledge.

Reader One: [13]At the same time, they also learn to be idle, going from house to house; they are not only idle, but are also gossips and busybodies, saying things they shouldn't say. [14]Therefore, I want younger women to marry, have children, manage their households, and give the adversary no opportunity to accuse us. [15]For some have already turned away to follow Satan. [16]If any believing woman has widows, she should help them, and the church should not be burdened, so that it can help those who are genuinely widows.

Reader Two: [17]The elders who are good leaders should be considered worthy of an ample honorarium, especially those who work hard at preaching and teaching. [18]For the Scripture says:

Reader Three: You must not muzzle an ox that is threshing grain, and, The laborer is worthy of his wages.

Reader Two: [19]Don't accept an accusation against an elder unless it is supported by two or three witnesses. [20]Publicly rebuke those who sin, so that the rest will also be afraid. [21]I solemnly charge you, before God and Christ Jesus and the elect angels, to observe these things without prejudice, doing nothing out of favoritism.

Reader One: [22]Don't be too quick to lay hands on anyone, and don't share in the sins of others. Keep yourself pure. [23]Don't continue drinking only water, but use a little wine because of your stomach and your frequent illnesses. [24]Some people's sins are evident, going before them to judgment, but the sins of others follow them. [25]Likewise, good works are obvious, and those that are not obvious cannot remain hidden.

Reader Three: 6 All who are under the yoke as slaves must regard their own masters to be worthy of all respect, so that God's name and His teaching will not be blasphemed. [2]And those who have believing masters should not be disrespectful to them because they are brothers, but should serve them better, since those who benefit from their service are believers and dearly loved.

1 Timothy 5:1–6:2

Questions for Interaction

1. When was the last time that you were in a nursing home? How did you feel about being there?

2. How is Timothy instructed to treat the genders and ages (vv. 1–2)?

3. How do you react to the idea that a person who does not provide for family (including older parents) is "worse than an unbeliever" (v. 8)?

4. How should the church care for widows who are really in need? What conditions need to be present and then how should the church take care of her (vv. 9–10)?

Leader
Refer to the Summary and Study Notes at the end of this session as needed. If 30 minutes is not enough time to answer all of the questions in this section, conclude the Bible Study by answering question 7.

5. Why are church elders to receive "an ample honorarium" (v. 17)?

   ○ Because of their age.
   ○ Because handling the church business is a difficult job.
   ○ Because their work takes time away from their family.
   ○ Because they are equipping the church for ministry.
   ○ Other _____.

6. What is the principle in Paul's instructions for slaves that would apply today to employer/employee relationships (6:1–2)? How does this relate to your work situation?

7. What do you need to change in your relationships with others so that God is glorified and not "blasphemed" (6:1)?

Going Deeper   If your group has time and/or wants a challenge, go on to this question.

---

8. What should be the Christian's/church's response to the welfare issue?

 Caring Time Apply the Lesson and Pray for One Another (15 minutes)

Come together now for a time of encouragement and prayer. Share your responses to the following questions, and then take turns offering prayer requests, concerns and praises.

1. What is the biggest issue or problem you are facing in the coming week that our group needs to pray for?

2. Who in your church needs some help that you or your group can provide?

3. What will you do this week individually or as a group to fill this need?

Leader
Encourage the group members to invite new people to the group. Remind them that this group is for learning and sharing, but it is also for reaching out to others. Close the group prayer by thanking God for each group member and the time that you share together in community.

NEXT WEEK *Today Paul showed us how to put love into action, as he addressed the issues of how to treat widows, elders and slaves. We were reminded that our conduct should always glorify God and be a witness to our beliefs. In the coming week, be sure to follow through on your answer to question 3 in the Caring Time. Next week we will focus on the love of money and the danger that distraction can pose to our faith.*

Summary: In this passage, Paul continues his instructions to Timothy. He makes comments on Timothy's relationship to older and younger men and women (5:1–2), on the question of widows (5:3–16), on the issue of elders (5:17–25) and then ends with a few words to slaves who are Christians (6:1–2).

5:1 *rebuke/exhort.* Timothy will have to confront older men over the issue of false teaching. Paul tells him how to do it. It is not by means of harsh "rebuke"; instead, he is to "earnestly petition" them.

5:3 *widows.* The early church—following the pattern of the Jewish nation before them—was committed to caring for those women who had lost their husbands (Deut. 24:17,19–21; Ps. 68:5; Isa. 1:17; Acts 6:1–6; 9:36–41; James 1:27).

5:4 The first group of widows who do not qualify for help are those who have family and friends who can care for them (vv. 8,16). Greek law stated that children were legally bound to support their parents. Paul's reason is that care of parents is one way to carry out one's religious duties. Children will "repay" the parent or grandparent for care given to them when they were young. Paul points out that this pleases God.

5:5–6 Paul next contrasts two types of widows: those who have put their hope in God (v. 5) and those who by their sensual living give no evidence of trusting God to meet their needs (v. 6). The first group is really "all alone" and so must trust God. The second group is "self-indulgent." In the first century it was very difficult for single women to support themselves. There were few jobs open to them, and so some were driven to prostitution. It may be that Paul is contrasting those women who refuse to be compromised (and so put their trust in God) with those women who live by sensual means (whether in actual prostitution or by being involved with a particular man).

5:9 *60 years old.* In the first century, 60 was considered the age of retirement and the point at which "old age" began. It was also considered to be the age beyond which remarriage was not a real possibility.

5:13 *saying things they shouldn't.* Their behavior had become the grounds on which others were speaking evil of the church. Paul continues in his concern that the church not be judged negatively by the surrounding culture.

5:18 Paul justifies his assertion that elders deserve remuneration by the community by means of two citations, one from the Old Testament (Deut. 25:4) and the other from Jesus (Luke 10:7).

5:19–20 Paul next addresses the matter of discipline. He says two things. First, no unsubstantiated charge is to be made about an elder, and second, if valid charges are made, those found guilty are to be rebuked publicly—serving to warn other elders who are in error as well as the whole church.

5:21 It is important that this rule be applied entirely across the board, even to those elders who might have great influence within the community.

5:22 *to lay hands on anyone.* The ordination of elders to office. *don't share in the sins of others.* Paul's comments on how to replace elders (do this carefully, since the sins of some are not apparent) lead him to make another "aside" to Timothy. Timothy must make sure his own life stays in order.

The Love of Money

Scripture 1 Timothy 6:3–10

LAST WEEK *How we treat others and take care of those in need was the focus of last week's session. We specifically discussed taking care of widows, honoring church leaders, providing for our own families and respecting our employers. Today we will study the root of the problems in the Ephesian church—the love of money. The love of money and the unhealthy pursuit of it can weaken our faith and cause damage to our relationships with business associates, friends and family.*

 Ice-Breaker Connect With Your Group (15 minutes)

Money—it is something we all need to survive. Making money and using it to live is an important part of our lives. But when it becomes the main motivation for all we do, as it did with the Ephesian elders, we know we must turn back to God and reevaluate our priorities. Take turns sharing some of your thoughts and unique life experiences with money.

Leader
Introduce and welcome new group members. If there are no new members, choose one or more of the Ice-Breaker questions to get started. If there are new members, then discuss all of the questions.

1. What was the first job you ever had? How much money did you make?

2. What ministries would you support if money were no object?

3. How much monetary cushion would you need to feel comfortable, content and secure?

   ○ Under $1,000.
   ○ Two weeks' income.
   ○ Two months' income.
   ○ Six months' income.
   ○ One year's income.
   ○ Five years' income.
   ○ Other _____.

4. Which of the following items would make you feel the most financially secure?

- ○ Savings account with six months income.
- ○ Life insurance worth five years income.
- ○ Investments worth two years income.
- ○ Great Health insurance.
- ○ A home that is paid off.
- ○ A job you like and feels secure.
- ○ A reliable vehicle that is paid off.
- ○ Parents that will support you in a crisis.
- ○ Other _____.

Bible Study Read Scripture and Discuss (30 minutes)

Leader
Ask two members of the group, selected ahead of time, to read aloud the Scripture passage. Then discuss the Questions for Interaction, dividing into subgroups of three to six for deeper and more personal interaction.

As the problems with leaders in the church are being identified, it becomes clear in this section of Scripture what the motivation of the false teachers is: money. The love of caused these erring teachers to stray from the faith. Read 1 Timothy 6:3–10 and see how the love of money can lead anyone into ruin and destruction.

The Love of Money

Reader One: Teach and encourage these things. ³If anyone teaches other doctrine and does not agree with the sound teaching of our Lord Jesus Christ and with the teaching that promotes godliness, ⁴he is conceited, understanding nothing, but having a sick interest in disputes and arguments over words.

Reader Two: From these come envy, quarreling, slanders, evil suspicions, ⁵and constant disagreement among men whose minds are depraved and deprived of the truth, who imagine that godliness is a way to material gain. ⁶But godliness with contentment is a great gain.

Reader One: ⁷For we brought nothing into the world,
and we can take nothing out.
⁸But if we have food and clothing,
we will be content with these.

Reader Two: ⁹But those who want to be rich fall into temptation, a trap, and many foolish and harmful desires, which plunge people into ruin and destruction. ¹⁰For the love of money is a root of all kinds of evil, and by craving it, some have wandered away from the faith and pierced themselves with many pains.

1 Timothy 6:3–10

Questions for Interaction

Leader
Refer to the Summary and Study Notes at the end of this session as needed. If you find that 30 minutes is not enough time to answer all of the questions in this section, conclude the Bible Study by answering question 7.

1. What is one principle about money you can remember learning from your parents or other adults?

2. Which statement best reflects your feelings about money?

   ○ Help! I need some more.
   ○ I have all the money I need.
   ○ I want more and more money.
   ○ There can't be too much money.
   ○ If I just had a little more money then I would be happy.
   ○ Money is not a big thing in my life.
   ○ Other _____.

3. What is the difference between enjoying money and being a lover of money (see also 6:17)? What guidelines are important to keep you from being a lover of money?

4. How would you compare the motivation of the false teachers to followers of Christ today?

   ○ Deep down we are all like this.
   ○ Most aren't this way.
   ○ I don't really see the problem.
   ○ Nothing much has changed.
   ○ Other _____.

5. Is there anything wrong with wanting to be rich (vv. 9–10)? Describe the differences between enjoying money and loving money.

6. What happens to some Christians when they are consumed with the "love of money" (v. 10)? Has there ever been a time in your life when you have been tempted to be a "lover" of money? What are some of the pitfalls you perceive?

7. How can you honor God with your money or your lack of money? How can you seek to be content with exactly what you have?

Going Deeper   If your group has time and/or wants a challenge, go on to this question.

8. What are some recent news events that illustrate the statement, "the love of money is a root of all kinds of evil" (v. 10)?

Caring Time
Apply the Lesson and Pray for One Another (15 minutes)

Leader
Make sure to reserve at least 15 minutes for this time of prayer, encouragement and affirmation. Continue to encourage the group members to invite new people to the group.

After sharing your responses to the following questions, close by praying for one another and for the concerns that have been shared. You may want to have the person you are praying for sit in the middle of the group and have everyone place a hand on the person as you pray.

1. Name some things that you value that money cannot buy.

2. On a scale of 1 (not at all) to 10 (completely), how content are you with your financial situation? How would you like it to change?

3. What is your biggest "temptation" and "trap" when it comes to money?

4. How can the group help to strengthen and encourage you as you seek to honor God with your money?

NEXT WEEK *Today we saw how no one seems to be immune from the love of money, not even church leaders. We discussed how money is not evil, but when the love of money becomes the motivation for all we do, then it becomes a dangerous problem. In the coming week, take a look at your checkbook and evaluate how it reflects your faith and values. Then ask the Holy Spirit to help you discern what changes you should make. Next week we will see how Paul encourages young Timothy to live a life that honors and glorifies God.*

Summary: Paul now summarizes the problem of false teachers and Timothy's role in dealing with them. In the process, he provides more details about false teachers. It turns out that they are motivated by pride, a love of arguments and greed (vv. 3–5). However, what really ought to motivate us, Paul says, is "godliness with contentment" (vv. 6–10).

6:3 *other doctrine.* Paul returns to the theme with which he began his letter (1:3). The false teachers have departed from the teaching of Jesus (1:10; 4:6). *the sound teaching of our Lord Jesus Christ.* This is their error. They have departed from the teaching of Jesus. This statement seems to indicate that early in the life of the church, the teachings of Jesus were collected and taught. The first gospels were probably written around the time of this letter.

6:4 *he is conceited, understanding nothing.* This is the first thing Paul says about these teachers. They are swollen with pride despite the fact they are really quite ignorant. *sick interest.* Literally, "being sick or diseased." This sort of "sickness" stands in sharp contrast to the sound (or "healthy") instruction of verse 3. *From these come.* Paul identifies two negative results of this sick preoccupation with word battles. First, it produces strife within the church, and second, it brings about a kind of corruption or decay to the minds of the teachers themselves. *Envy.* The word refers to resentful awareness of the advantage of others and the desire to possesses the same advantages. (Love does not envy. 1 Cor. 13:4). *quarreling.* This is more than just "disputes." This is literally a "battle of words," which Paul sharply criticizes. *slanders, evil suspicions.* This quarreling drives people to tell lies about and ascribe bad motives to one another.

6:5 *minds are depraved.* "Mind" refers to one's whole way of thinking. *deprived of the truth.* Such corruption results in the loss of the very truth of the Gospel. *godliness is a way to material gain.* As Paul has hinted in 3:3 and 8, the bottom line motivation of these false teachers is the money they make from their teaching. Paul does not consider it wrong for a person to be paid for teaching (5:17–18), but he is incensed when greed is the main motivation for ministry.

6:6 This verse stands in immediate contrast to the last words in verse 5, with a striking play on terms. They think godliness "is a way to material gain." *contentment.* This was a favorite word of the Stoic philosophers from whom Paul borrowed it. (Zeno, the founder of this philosophical school, came from Tarsus, Paul's hometown.) This word refers to a person who is not impacted by circumstances. Such a person is self-contained and thus able to rise above all conditions. For Paul, however, this sort of contentment was derived from the Lord (Phil. 4:11).

6:9 *temptation.* Greed causes people to notice and desire things that harm them, that they might not otherwise have paid attention to.

6:10 *For the love of money is a root of all kinds of evil.* Paul is probably quoting a well-known proverb in order to support the assertion he makes in verse 9 that the desire for money leads to ruin. This verse is often misquoted as "money is the root of all evil." While Paul clearly sees the danger of money, he is not contending that all evil can be traced to avarice. *some have wandered.* Here is the problem. Some of the false teachers have given in to the temptation to riches. They were probably once good leaders in the church but they got caught by Satan (4:1–2), became enamored with speculative ideas (vv. 3–5), and in the end were pulled down by their love for money.

Pursue Right Living

Scripture 1 Timothy 6:11–21

LAST WEEK *In our time together last week we saw how the love of money was the driving force behind the false teachers. This love for financial gain caused church leaders to stray from their faith and do evil things in the sight of God. Today we will see the apostle Paul encourage Timothy on how to live a life free from greed, avoiding the teachings, behavior and attitudes of these men who have caused chaos in the church.*

Ice-Breaker Connect With Your Group (15 minutes)

We all need encouragement from time to time—to continue things that we are doing right, to do things that would enhance our lives, and sometimes to step out of our comfort zone to take a risk. Take turns sharing your experiences with risk-taking.

Leader
Choose one, two or all three of the Ice-Breaker questions. Be sure to welcome and introduce new group members.

1. When you were growing up, did your parents overprotect you or did they push you to go beyond your limits?

2. What motto best describes your level of risk-taking?

○ Better safe than sorry.
○ No! The water is too cold.
○ Here goes nothing.
○ Only if the conditions are right.
○ Go for it!
○ Other _____.

3. What sport or recreational activity would you like to try if you knew you wouldn't get injured?

- ○ Mountain climbing.
- ○ Hang gliding.
- ○ Ski jumping.
- ○ Sun bathing.
- ○ Gymnastics.
- ○ Swimming with sharks.
- ○ Sing in the choir.
- ○ Other _____

 Bible Study Read Scripture and Discuss (30 minutes)

Leader
Select three members of the group ahead of time to read aloud the Scripture passage. Then discuss the Questions for Interaction, dividing into subgroups of three to six.

As Paul deals with the problems caused by the false teachers and the ways in which they have deceived the people, he follows up with an encouragement to Timothy. Paul advises him to "run," "pursue," "fight" and "take hold." He wants Timothy to flee from the elders' false teaching, lifestyle and attitudes. Read 1 Timothy 6:11–21 and note the kind of life that pleases God and brings honor to his name.

Pursue Right Living

Reader One: ^{11}Now you, man of God, run from these things;
      but pursue righteousness, godliness, faith,
      love, endurance, and gentleness.
    ^{12}Fight the good fight for the faith;
      take hold of eternal life,
      to which you were called
      and have made a good confession
      before many witnesses.

Reader Two: ^{13}In the presence of God, who gives life to all, and before Christ Jesus, who gave a good confession before Pontius Pilate, I charge you ^{14}to keep the commandment without spot or blame until the appearing of our Lord Jesus Christ, ^{15}which God will bring about in His own time. He is
      the blessed and only Sovereign,
      the King of kings,
      and the Lord of lords,
    ^{16}the only One who has immortality,
      dwelling in unapproachable light,
      whom none of mankind has seen or can see,
      to whom be honor and eternal might.
      Amen.

Reader Three: [17]Instruct those who are rich in the present age not to be arrogant or to set their hope on the uncertainty of wealth, but on God, who richly provides us with all things to enjoy. [18]Instruct them to do good, to be rich in good works, to be generous, willing to share, [19]storing up for themselves a good foundation for the age to come, so that they may take hold of life that is real.

Reader One: [20]Timothy, guard what has been entrusted to you, avoiding irreverent, empty speech and contradictions from the "knowledge" that falsely bears that name.

Reader Two: [21]By professing it, some people have deviated from the faith.

Reader One: Grace be with all of you.

1 Timothy 6:11–21

Questions for Interaction

1. Who is your spiritual mentor (coach)? Who gives you encouragement?

2. If you were Timothy, how would you feel after reading this letter from Paul?

  ○ Overwhelmed with the task.
  ○ Where's Paul when you need him.
  ○ Empowered.
  ○ Confident.
  ○ Ready for a fight.
  ○ Other _____.

Leader
Refer to the Summary and Study Notes at the end of this session as needed. If 30 minutes is not enough time to answer all of the questions in this section, conclude the Bible Study by answering questions 6 and 7.

3. What is Timothy being asked to run away from? What is he being asked to pursue (v. 11)?

4. What struggles is Timothy going through? In what areas are his struggles similar to your own struggles?

5. In the previous passage (6:3–10), Paul focuses his attention on the love of money and how it can lead to evil. What does he say in verses 17–19 about wealth?

6. What grade would God give your life as it relates to verses 18–19, and why?

  ○ A
  ○ B
  ○ C
  ○ D
  ○ F
  ○ Incomplete.

7. Are you wandering spiritually, or are you in hot pursuit of the qualities in verse 11? Which quality do you especially want to develop in your life?

Going Deeper   If your group has time and/or wants a challenge, go on to this question.

---

8. What does it mean to "fight the good fight for the faith" (v. 12)? What does this tell you about what we must expect in the Christian life?

Caring Time   Apply the Lesson and Pray for One Another (15 minutes)

Praying for one another is a great help in time of need or concern. Take time now to share your responses to the questions below. Then share prayer requests and close with a time of prayer.

1. Did you feel more like a winner or loser in your "fight for the faith" (v. 12) this past week?

2. As you think back over your spiritual journey, when were you thrust into a position for which you felt totally inadequate? What did God teach you from this experience?

3. What is the most important truth you learned from 1 Timothy? How will you apply this truth to your life?

Leader
Have you started working with your group about the group's mission—perhaps by sharing the dream of multiplying into two groups by the end of this study of 1 and 2 Timothy?

NEXT WEEK *This book serves as backdrop for how anyone of us can "suffer the shipwreck" of our faith (1:19). Paul provides us with a solid understanding of what to do when we encounter false teaching, greed and pride. He also encourages us to live the way God intended by pursuing righteousness, godliness, faith, love, endurance and gentleness. In the coming week, ask the Holy Spirit to help you apply the truth that you shared in question 3 in the Caring Time. Next week we will open the letter of 2 Timothy, which was written two to five years after 1 Timothy. In this next letter, Paul appeals to Timothy to remain loyal to Christ, even in the face of suffering.*

Summary: Every time Paul brings up the problem of the false teachers he then immediately follows up with a word of exhortation to Timothy. So far he has done this three times. He followed up his first discussion of the false teachers in 1:3–7 with his words to Timothy in 1:18–19. (Verses 8–17 are a parenthetical statement.) He did the same thing in 4:1–5, which he followed up by 4:6–16. Now, having discussed the false teachers in 6:3–10, even though he has more to say about wealth (see vv. 17–19), he injects verses 11–16 in which he makes a final appeal to Timothy.

6:11 *Now you.* Once again Paul contrasts Timothy to the false teachers. *man of God.* Paul draws this term from the Old Testament where it was used to refer to various servants of God who represented God and spoke his word (Deut. 33:1; Josh. 14:6; 1 Sam. 9:6; Neh. 12:24). This title emphasizes Timothy's role as a minister of God in contrast to the false teachers who have ceased to be servants of God. *run from these things.* Timothy is to move with haste and intentionality away from not only greed, but from the speculative, contentious doctrines of the false teachers. *pursue.* Timothy is to "run away from" the behavior and attitudes of the false teachers, and instead go toward ("pursue") those virtues that reflect the Gospel. Paul names six traits that Timothy is to cultivate. *righteousness.* This can be translated "integrity." It refers to upright conduct (Phil. 1:11). *godliness.* This is the same word that is used in 3:16 and 4:7–8; 6:5–6. It refers to a person's relationship to God, especially as it shows itself in outward behavior. This word might also be translated "piety"—though "piety" has a somewhat negative connotation today, which is not the sense of the word as it is used here. *faith, love.* These two virtues regularly appear together in the Pastoral Epistles (1:5; 2:15; 4:12; 2 Tim. 2:22; Titus 2:2). *endurance.* Paul is not urging a passive attitude to life but rather a kind of active, overcoming constancy in the face of trial. *gentleness.* This is the kind of spirit in people that means they do not defend themselves, but yet they are deeply concerned when others are wronged (Gal. 5:23; Eph. 4:2; Col. 3:12). It is characterized by even temper and kindness toward others.

6:12 *Fight the good fight.* Paul uses an athletic metaphor to encourage Timothy to persevere in the faith. The verb tense emphasizes that this is an ongoing struggle. *take hold of eternal life.* The focus shifts from the contest to the prize. A person can grasp eternal life through a single act, yet there needs to be a continuing awareness of the goal of our salvation. *to which you were called.* Paul gives Timothy two reasons for waging this fight. This is the first. God has "called" him to eternal life. *a good confession.* This is the second reason. He has publicly acknowledged this call. It is not certain to which event in his Christian life Paul refers, though he may well have had in mind Timothy's baptism (when he publicly declared his faith in Christ).

6:14 *commandment.* It is not clear just what "command" Timothy is being charged to keep. It has been understood to mean the imperatives in verses 11–12, his baptismal or ordination vows (depending upon how verse 12 is interpreted), the Christian faith in general, or his own faith and ministry (as in 4:16). Probably the latter is intended. It fits with the purpose of the whole letter and goes along with Paul's final charge to Timothy in verse 20.

6:15 *in His own time.* In this verse, Paul

makes two statements about the Second Coming. First, it is certain ("God will bring it about") and second, it will come about when God judges the moment to be right ("in his own time").

6:17 *those who are rich.* This is the only place in his letters that Paul addresses the wealthy directly. His consistent "commandment" is that the rich share their wealth with the poor (Rom. 12:8,13; 2 Cor. 9:6–15). *not to be arrogant or to set their hope on ... wealth.* These are the twin dangers of wealth—that it will cause people to think themselves to be better than others, and that they might put their trust in their riches (and not in God). *to enjoy.* But

Paul is no ascetic. That the wealthy should not place confidence in their wealth does not carry with it an attitude of total rejection.

6:20 *entrusted to you.* Paul uses a legal term here. It refers to a treasure that has been given over to a banker (or to a friend) for safekeeping. The "treasure" given Timothy is his call to minister in Ephesus, which involved resisting the false teachers, living a model Christian life and faithfully proclaiming the Gospel.

6:21 *Grace be with all of you.* Paul ends with an uncharacteristically brief benediction. "You" is plural, indicating once again that this was a public letter to be read by the whole church.

Encouragement to Be Faithful

Scripture 2 Timothy 1:1–12

LAST WEEK *We concluded our study of 1 Timothy in last week's session. We were encouraged to run away from evil and "fight the good fight for the faith" (1 Tim. 6:12). As we open the letter of 2 Timothy the emphasis has changed. It is several years later now and Paul is in prison and facing execution. Paul desires for Timothy to come and be with him, and he encourages him to be faithful to Christ and his ministry (and to Paul himself). The apostle's desire is to transfer his leadership to Timothy.*

 Ice-Breaker Connect With Your Group (15 minutes)

Leader
Welcome and introduce new group members. Choose one, two or all three of the Ice-Breaker questions, depending on your group's needs.

All of us carry the traits of our parents, and we have a heritage that helps to shape us. When Paul wrote this letter he reminded Timothy of the contribution that his grandmother, Lois, and his mother, Eunice, made to Timothy's character. It is sometimes helpful to remember where we come from. Take turns sharing some of your history and background.

1. The physical trait that I inherited from my mom or dad is (check all that apply):

   ❍ Nose.
   ❍ Eyes.
   ❍ Skin.
   ❍ Body shape.
   ❍ Hair.
   ❍ Mouth shape.
   ❍ Ears.
   ❍ Other _____.

2. What relative or friend would you like to see that you haven't seen in a while?

3. Of all your friends in high school, who are still your friends today?

Bible Study Read Scripture and Discuss (30 minutes)

As this passage from 2 Timothy begins, we find Paul in a Roman prison cell—cold, bored and lonely. He realizes that he is at the end of his ministry and uses this letter to encourage Timothy to remain loyal to Christ. This letter also serves as a powerful testimony of the rich relationship Paul has with God through Jesus. Read 2 Timothy 1:1–12 and note Paul's unwavering faith in spite of his circumstances.

Leader
Ask two group members, selected ahead of time, to read out loud the Scripture passage. Then discuss the Questions for Interaction, dividing into subgroups of three to six.

Encouragement to Be Faithful

Reader One: 1 Paul, an apostle of Christ Jesus by God's will, for the promise of life in Christ Jesus:

²To Timothy, my dearly loved child.
Grace, mercy, and peace from God the Father and Christ Jesus our Lord.

³I thank God, whom I serve with a clear conscience as my forefathers did, when I constantly remember you in my prayers night and day. ⁴Remembering your tears, I long to see you so that I may be filled with joy, ⁵clearly recalling your sincere faith that first lived in your grandmother Lois, then in your mother Eunice, and that I am convinced is in you also.

Reader Two: ⁶Therefore, I remind you to keep ablaze the gift of God that is in you through the laying on of my hands. ⁷For God has not given us a spirit of fearfulness, but one of power, love, and sound judgment.

Reader One: ⁸So don't be ashamed of the testimony about our Lord, or of me His prisoner. Instead, share in suffering for the gospel, relying on the power of God,

Reader Two: ⁹who has saved us
and called us with a holy calling,
not according to our works
but according to His own purpose and grace,
which was given to us in Christ Jesus
before time began.
¹⁰This has now been made evident
through the appearing of our Savior Christ Jesus,
who has abolished death
and has brought life and immortality to light
through the gospel.

Reader One: ¹¹For this gospel I was appointed a herald, apostle, and teacher, ¹²and that is why I suffer these things. But I am not ashamed, because I know whom I have believed and am persuaded that He is able to guard what has been entrusted to me until that day.

2 Timothy 1:1–12

Questions for Interaction

Leader
Refer to the Summary and Study Notes at the end of this session as needed. If 30 minutes is not enough time to answer all of the questions in this section, conclude the Bible Study by answering question 7.

1. Who has inspired you in the faith in the way that Lois and Eunice inspired Timothy?

2. According to verses 3–4, Paul viewed Timothy as ... (check the best one):

   ○ An enemy.
   ○ A casual friend.
   ○ A good friend.
   ○ Dearly loved friend.
   ○ Business partner.
   ○ Other _____.

3. What does Paul encourage Timothy to do when he tells him to "keep ablaze the gift of God" (v. 6) that is within him?

4. How does Paul challenge Timothy not to be timid and shy (vv. 5–7)? Considering that this is an area of weakness in Timothy's life, is Paul asking too much of him (see notes on v. 7)?

5. How do you think it made Paul feel when everyone in Asia deserted him?

6. At what point in your life have you ever felt deserted and alone?

7. Have you been shy or timid about sharing Jesus with others? What can help keep you from being ashamed of the Gospel (v. 12)?

Going Deeper   If your group has time and/or wants a challenge, go on to this question.

8. What does it mean to have "a holy calling" (v. 9)? Do all Christians have a holy calling, or is that reserved for a select few?

Caring Time Apply the Lesson and Pray for One
Another (15 minutes)

Use this time to encourage, challenge and pray for one another and your own special concerns. Take turns sharing responses to the following questions. Then close with a time of group prayer, asking God to give you the strength to keep praying for those you've almost given up on.

1. What do you look forward to most about these meetings?

2. Who has developed (mentored) you in the faith? How would you like to thank God for this person?

3. Who are you bringing along in the faith? How are you investing yourself in that person's life? If the answer is "no one," who is God challenging you to approach?

Leader
Have you identified your Timothy? Do you know someone in the group that could be a leader for a new small group when your group finishes this study and divides? How could you encourage and mentor this person?

NEXT WEEK *Today we saw Paul encourage and challenge Timothy to live up to his "holy calling." We were reminded how important it is that someone walk alongside us as we follow Jesus—someone who will mentor us, love us as a friend and work with us in spreading the Gospel. If you are not mentoring someone in the faith, ask God to reveal someone to you. In the coming week, reflect on 2 Timothy 1:1–12 and its significance. Next week Paul continues this theme of being faithful in the face of persecution and adversity.*

Summary: This epistle is quite a different letter than the first one Paul wrote to his young companion. Paul is now in prison, and conditions are awful. He is alone, in chains and wants Timothy with him. So he writes this letter asking him to come. But being who he is, Paul can't just write with a request. He uses the opportunity to say some important things to Timothy about his ministry. In the first part of the letter, Paul follows his brief (and typical) salutation (vv. 1–2) with a thanksgiving (vv. 3–5) and an exhortation (vv. 6–8). Then beginning in 1:6, he touches on what will emerge as the central themes of this letter. Paul appeals to Timothy to remain loyal to Christ, to him and to Timothy's own ministry, even in the face of suffering.

1:1 *an apostle of Christ Jesus.* At first glance it is surprising that Paul uses his title in such a personal letter. However, as in 1 Timothy, he is making his appeal in this letter as an apostle. This time his appeal is to Timothy. He urges him in strong terms to maintain his loyalty to him and to the Gospel, despite the suffering this may entail. There may be a second reason why Paul uses his title. Others will probably read this letter. In particular, Timothy will need to show it to the elders in Ephesus when he tells them that Paul wants him to leave and go to Rome.

1:3 *as my forefathers did.* Paul also stands squarely in the Old Testament tradition of faith of his forebearers (in contrast to the false teachers who had, effectively, left the faith). *I constantly remember you.* Paul prayed regularly, and in those prayers he always remembered Timothy.

1:4 *Remembering your tears.* Paul is probably remembering when they parted the last time; he had to go on to Macedonia while Timothy stayed in Ephesus (see Acts 20:37 for a similar situation). *I long to see you.* This is the main reason he writes this letter: to urge Timothy to join him (4:9). *joy.* Once again, as he did in Philippians, Paul sounds a note of joy even though he is in prison.

1:5 *Eunice.* Timothy's mother was a Jewish Christian (Acts 16:1). His father was a Gentile, who probably was not a believer.

1:6 *keep ablaze.* Literally, "rekindle." Paul uses the image of a fire, not to suggest that the gift of ministry has "gone out," but that it needs constant stirring up so that it always burns brightly. *the gift of God.* Paul reminds Timothy not only of his spiritual roots (the faith of his mother and grandmother), but of the gift of the Spirit (*charisma* in Greek) he has been given for ministry.

1:7 Paul makes this sort of appeal because Timothy is not a forceful person. *power, love, and sound judgment.* The gift the Spirit gave Timothy leads not to "fearfulness," but to these positive characteristics.

1:8 Timothy is able to do what Paul here calls him to do because he has been given power, love and sound judgment (v. 7). *ashamed of the testimony about our Lord.* The Gospel message about a crucified Savior was not immediately popular in the first-century world. The Greeks laughed at the idea that the Messiah could be a convicted criminal, and that God was so weak that he would allow his own Son to die. And the Jews could not conceive of a Messiah (whom they knew to be all-powerful) dying on a cross (which they felt disqualified him from acceptance by God). It was not easy to preach the Gospel in the face of such scorn. *of me.* When Paul was rearrested, his friends deserted him (1:15). He does not want Timothy to do the same. *His prisoner.* Paul may be in a Roman jail, but he knows that he is not a prisoner of Caesar. He is, and has long been, a willing prisoner of Jesus (Eph. 3:1; 4:1; Philem. 1,9). *share in.* In fact, rather than being ashamed of the Gospel (or of Paul and his suffering), Timothy ought to share in this suffering. *suffering.* Paul understands from his own experience (and from that of Jesus) that suffering is part of what it means to follow the Gospel (3:12; Rom. 8:17; 2 Cor. 4:7–15; Phil. 1:12,29; Col. 1:24; 1 Thess. 1:6; 2:14; 3:4).

1:9 *has saved us.* Timothy can face suffering because he has already experienced salvation. This is an accomplished fact. *grace.* God's work of salvation depends wholly on "grace" (his unmerited favor lavished on his creation), not "according to our works." This grace, which was in place "before time began," is "given to us in Christ Jesus" (Eph. 1:4).

1:10 *appearing.* The Greek word is *epiphaneia* (from which the English word "epiphany" is derived). It refers here to the "manifestation" of God's grace through the incarnation of Christ. *Savior.* This was a common title in the first century. It was applied to the Roman emperor (in his role as head of the state religion) and to various redeemer-gods in the mystery religions. Christians came to see that Jesus was the one and only Savior. *death/life.* Jesus' work of salvation is described in his twofold act of destroying the power of death over people (death no longer has the final word) and bringing resurrection life in its place.

1:12 *I am not ashamed.* The fact that he is in prison brings no shame to Paul, despite how others might view it.

Encouragement to Be Faithful (cont.)

Scripture 2 Timothy 1:13–2:13

LAST WEEK *We began our study together last week with Paul's encouragement to Timothy to be faithful even in the midst of turmoil. His prayer for Timothy is that he will not be discouraged by the coming persecution of the church, and that he will not abandon the faith as many were in Asia. Rather, he encourages him to not "be ashamed of the testimony about our Lord or of me His prisoner" (1:8). As we study this week, Paul continues to give Timothy encouragement to remain strong.*

 Ice-Breaker Connect With Your Group (15 minutes)

In times of struggle and hardship, it helps so much to have someone who encourages us to remain strong. In the passage for today, Paul appeals to his spiritual "son" Timothy, to be strong in his own difficulty. Take turns sharing your experiences with hard times and the people who have helped you.

Leader
Choose one or two of the Ice-Breaker questions. If you have a new group member you may want to do all three. Remember to stick closely to the three-part agenda and the time allowed for each segment.

1. Who in your life has really been there for you in the hard times?

   ○ Spouse.
   ○ Sibling.
   ○ Coach.
   ○ Teacher.
   ○ Spiritual leader.
   ○ Friend.
   ○ Other _____.
   How did this person help you?

2. When was the last time you needed help due to a car problem? What happened?

3. Who would you call for help if you got thrown in jail tonight?

Bible Study Read Scripture and Discuss (30 minutes)

Leader

Ask two group members, selected ahead of time, to read aloud the Scripture passage. Then discuss the Questions for Interaction, dividing into subgroups of three to six.

It is easy at times to give up in a difficult situation. We have the tendency to wonder, "What good is it for me to stand strong?" We are encouraged in this passage, not only by the example of Paul and the hardship he is suffering, but because of the tremendous promise given in 2:11–13 for all who endure to the end. Read 2 Timothy 1:13–2:13 and note what this promise is.

Encouragement to Be Faithful

Reader One: [13]Hold on to the pattern of sound teaching that you have heard from me, in the faith and love that are in Christ Jesus. [14]Guard, through the Holy Spirit who lives in us, that good thing entrusted to you. [15]This you know: all those in Asia have turned away from me, including Phygelus and Hermogenes. [16]May the Lord grant mercy to the household of Onesiphorus, because he often refreshed me and was not ashamed of my chains. [17]On the contrary, when he was in Rome, he diligently searched for me and found me. [18]May the Lord grant that he obtain mercy from the Lord on that day. And you know how much he ministered at Ephesus.

Reader Two: 2 You, therefore, my child, be strong in the grace that is in Christ Jesus. [2]And what you have heard from me in the presence of many witnesses, commit to faithful men who will be able to teach others also.

[3]Share in suffering as a good soldier of Christ Jesus. [4]To please the recruiter, no one serving as a soldier gets entangled in the concerns of everyday life. [5]Also, if anyone competes as an athlete, he is not crowned unless he competes according to the rules. [6]It is the hardworking farmer who ought to be the first to get a share of the crops. [7]Consider what I say, for the Lord will give you understanding in everything.

Reader One: [8]Keep in mind Jesus Christ, risen from the dead, descended from David, according to my gospel. [9]For this I suffer, to the point of being bound like a criminal; but God's message is not bound. [10]This is why I endure all things for the elect: so that they also may obtain salvation, which is in Christ Jesus, with eternal glory. [11]This saying is trustworthy:

Reader Two: For if we have died with Him,
we will also live with Him;
[12]if we endure,
we will also reign with Him;
if we deny Him,
He will also deny us;
[13]if we are faithless,
He remains faithful,
for He cannot deny Himself.

2 Timothy 1:13–2:13

Questions for Interaction

Leader
Refer to the Summary and Study Notes at the end of this session as needed. If 30 minutes is not enough time to answer all of the questions in this section, conclude the Bible Study by answering question 7.

1. When you are discouraged, how do you usually respond?

   ○ I quit.
   ○ I eat.
   ○ I fight.
   ○ I run.
   ○ I get even.
   ○ I never get discouraged.
   ○ Other _____.

2. Where do you go for spiritual refreshment in times of discouragement (1:16–18)?

   ○ The Bible.
   ○ My pastor.
   ○ My best friend.
   ○ Mom.
   ○ Dad.
   ○ Church.
   ○ My group.
   ○ God.
   ○ Other _____.

3. Why is Paul concerned about Timothy being "strong" (2:1)? What pressures do you think he is facing?

4. Considering the persecution that the followers of Jesus are facing, what factor will ensure that the message of Jesus will live on (2:2)? Because Paul believes that he will be executed, what is of vital importance to him as he contemplates his death?

5. In spite of his suffering, what keeps Paul from giving up (2:8–10)? What has kept you going in times of suffering?

   ○ Belief in the cause.
   ○ Focusing on the goal.
   ○ Faith.
   ○ Other _____.

6. What encourages you the most in verses 11–13? What challenges you?

7. In what way(s) are you presently suffering? How are you dealing with it?

8. What do the examples of the soldier, athlete and farmer (2:3–7) teach about the Christian life? How would these illustrations encourage Timothy (and us) to steadfastly endure suffering?

 Caring Time Apply the Lesson and Pray for One Another (15 minutes)

The apostle Paul understood the importance of encouragement in the life of Timothy. Take time now to support and encourage one another through sharing and prayer.

Leader
Be sure that everyone is receiving prayer support as needed. Conclude the prayer time today by reading together 2:11–13.

1. How has God been at work in your life in the past week? In what area of your life do you need encouragement?

2. What pressure are you facing in this coming week that God desires you to be strong in? What is he calling you to do?

3. How can our group pray for you in the sufferings you mentioned in question 7? In what tangible way can we encourage and support you?

> **NEXT WEEK** *Today we considered the theme of being faithful in the face of persecution and adversity. We were reminded that sometimes we need others to help us keep going and not give up. In the coming week, reflect on today's passage and its significance, specifically meditating on the promise that we have in verses 11–13. What will you do this week in the face of adversity? Will you make excuses or will you stand strong? Next week we will focus on what happens when we disown Jesus and his suffering.*

Summary: In this lengthy section of Paul's letter from 1:3–2:13, he encourages Timothy to be faithful. In his first appeal (1:8–18), Paul challenges Timothy to remain faithful to both Christ and Paul. Timothy should take warning from those who have deserted the apostle Paul in his imprisonment. In Paul's second appeal (2:1–13), he admonishes his spiritual "son," Timothy, to be strong in his own hardships. Always in Paul's mind is his concern for the future of the Christian faith, as he calls Timothy to relay Paul's teachings to others—who in turn can instruct yet others (2:1).

1:13–18 Paul concludes the exhortation begun in 1:8, charging young Timothy to be loyal in his faith.

1:15 *Asia.* This reference is to what is now known as Asia Minor (which was then a Roman province), with the capital at Ephesus.

2:1 *grace.* Grace is the sphere within which the Christian lives and moves. It is the unmerited favor that God has shown us and the nature of God's continuing ministry in our lives. *in Christ Jesus.* The source of grace is union with Christ.

2:2 Just as the Gospel has been entrusted to Timothy (1:14; 1 Tim. 6:20), so he is to entrust it to others who, in turn, teach it to yet others. This whole process of "entrusting" is made doubly important by the fact that Paul will soon call Timothy to join him in Rome (which means that others will have to take over his teaching ministry in Ephesus).

2:3 *Share in suffering.* This Greek word is the same one used in 1:8 and so it should probably be translated "join with me in suffering" since this gives a better sense of what Paul is calling Timothy to do.

2:6 *to get a share of the crops.* In each of the three images there is the idea of reward.

2:8 First, Paul calls upon Timothy to "keep in mind" Jesus Christ. In particular, Paul notes two truths about Jesus: his resurrection and his lineage. What might these terse phrases say to Timothy? By pointing to the resurrection of Jesus, Paul may be reminding Timothy that in this way Jesus demonstrated that he is Lord over even death, and is thus able to strengthen his people in times of suffering (and give them victory over death too). By pointing to the fact that Jesus came from the line of David, Paul may be reminding Timothy that God fulfills his promises. (He did send the promised Messiah to Israel.) His lineage also shows that Jesus is truly human, one who could and did suffer. (Both facts are additional sources of confidence for Timothy.) These two phrases encompass the life of Jesus from incarnation (the seed of David) to exaltation (the throne of David).

2:9–10 Paul reminds Timothy again that his suffering is a result of his service to Jesus.

2:9 *criminal.* This is the term used for those who committed serious crimes (such as murder and theft). This must have been especially galling to Paul that he—a Roman citizen, innocent of any crime save preaching the Gospel of salvation—was classified as a common criminal.

2:10 *the elect.* God's chosen people. *may obtain salvation.* Paul's suffering will further the spread of the Gospel, through which men and women obtain salvation.

2:11 *saying is trustworthy.* Once again Paul uses the formula by which he introduces a quotation familiar to his readers (1 Tim. 1:15; 3:1; 4:9;

Titus 3:8). In the hymn or poem that follows, each line is introduced by an "if" clause which presents an action on the part of a Christian. The "then" clause shows the results of this action in relationship to Christ.

2:12 The middle two lines are the reason why Paul cites this hymn. They contain a promise and a warning coupled with a call to endure in the face of hardship—the key themes of this section of the letter.

Approved by God

Scripture 2 Timothy 2:14–26

> **LAST WEEK** *Last week's lesson was about having the determination to stay strong in the faith even though others are abandoning the Lord. This week Paul once again addresses the problem of the false teachers in the Ephesian church. He specifically warns against the "irreverent, empty speech" (v. 16) they are using. We will also see Paul encourage Timothy to "be diligent to present yourself approved to God, a worker who doesn't need to be ashamed" (v. 15).*

Ice-Breaker Connect With Your Group (15 minutes)

"Silence is golden" is a popular phrase that emphasizes how words can be used to bring strife and discord. We've probably all been affected in our lives by words that should never have been said. Take turns sharing your experiences with quarrelsome words.

Leader
Choose one, two or all three Ice-Breaker questions, depending on your group's needs.

1. As a child, what did you argue the most about with other children?

   ○ Who went first.
   ○ Who got more.
   ○ The fairness of an event.
   ○ Who got to sit in which seat.
   ○ Who was the tallest.
   ○ Who was the smartest.
   ○ Who was the strongest.
   ○ Whose dad was tougher.
   ○ Other _____.

2. What do you do when someone wants to argue with you?

3. What is one topic that's sure to provoke an argument at your family gatherings now?

- ○ Politics.
- ○ Religion.
- ○ Correcting one another.
- ○ Who was the tallest.
- ○ Who was the smartest.
- ○ Who was the strongest.
- ○ Whose dad was tougher.
- ○ Other _____.

Bible Study Read Scripture and Discuss (30 minutes)

Paul reminds us in today's passage that believers must avoid teachers that oppose the truth. Following deception can mislead even the strongest believers. Keeping close to the Gospel of truth is not a one-time event but something that must be done daily. Read 2 Timothy 2:14–26 and note the importance Paul places on the words we say.

Leader
Ask two group members, selected ahead of time, to read aloud the Scripture passage. Have one person read verses 14–19; and the other read verses 20–26. Then discuss the Questions for Interaction, dividing into subgroups of three to six.

Approved by God

Reader One: ¹⁴Remind them of these things, charging them before God not to fight about words; this is in no way profitable and leads to the ruin of the hearers. ¹⁵Be diligent to present yourself approved to God, a worker who doesn't need to be ashamed, correctly teaching the word of truth. ¹⁶But avoid irreverent, empty speech, for this will produce an even greater measure of godlessness. ¹⁷And their word will spread like gangrene, among whom are Hymenaeus and Philetus. ¹⁸They have deviated from the truth, saying that the resurrection has already taken place, and are overturning the faith of some. ¹⁹Nevertheless, God's solid foundation stands firm, having this inscription:

> The Lord knows those who are His, and
> Everyone who names the name of the Lord
> must turn away from unrighteousness.

Reader Two: ²⁰Now in a large house there are not only gold and silver bowls, but also those of wood and earthenware, some for special use, some for ordinary. ²¹So if anyone purifies himself from these things, he will be a special instrument, set apart, useful to the Master, prepared for every good work.

²²Flee from youthful passions, and pursue righteousness, faith, love, and peace, along with those who call on the Lord from a pure heart. ²³But reject foolish and ignorant disputes, knowing that they breed quarrels. ²⁴The Lord's slave must not quarrel, but must be gentle to everyone, able to teach, and patient, ²⁵instructing his opponents with gentleness. Perhaps God will grant them repentance to know the truth. ²⁶Then they may come to their senses and escape the Devil's trap, having been captured by him to do his will.

2 Timothy 2:14–26

Questions for Interaction

Leader
Refer to the Summary and Study Notes at the end of this session as needed. If 30 minutes is not enough time to answer all of the questions in this section, conclude the Bible Study by answering questions 6 and 7.

1. As a teenager, what warning do you wish you had listened to?

   ○ Don't smoke.
   ○ Don't run with scissors.
   ○ Study hard.
   ○ Obey traffic laws.
   ○ Don't stay out late.
   ○ Avoid certain people.
   ○ Don't drink and drive.
   ○ Other _____.

2. In verse 14, what warning does Paul give Christians? What is the difference between standing against false teaching and not fighting "about words"?

3. How would you describe these "false teachers" (vv. 14–18)? What has the false teaching about the resurrection done to the church?

4. What does Paul mean by "God's solid foundation" that stands firm in spite of error and false teaching (see notes on v. 19)? In what way does this challenge the church today?

5. For Timothy to clean up his life, what are some things that he needs to work on (vv. 22–25)?

6. Which characteristic listed in verse 22 do you most need to pursue in your life today?

   ○ Righteousness.
   ○ Faith.
   ○ Love.
   ○ Peace.
   ○ Purity.
   ○ Other _____.

7. When has the kind of repentance described in verse 25 led you to a deeper knowledge of the truth?

Going Deeper   If your group has time and/or wants a challenge, go on to this question.

---

8. How would you rewrite verses 20–21 in your own words? (Include some practical examples of how a person can purify him or herself.)

Caring Time Apply the Lesson and Pray for One Another (15 minutes)

Leader
Conclude the prayer time today by asking God for guidance in determining the future mission and outreach of this group.

Accountability between members in a small group is an essential ingredient in becoming all that God desires us to be. During this Caring Time, honestly reflect on your life and share what God asks you to share.

1. What do you appreciate the most about this group?

2. In what area of your life do you feel "captured" in the "Devil's trap" (v. 26)? What can this group do to help?

3. What will you do this week to "be diligent to present yourself approved to God, a worker who doesn't need to be ashamed, correctly teaching the word of truth" (v. 15)?

NEXT WEEK *Today we focused on the damage that words can do in our relationships with others and with God. We were reminded how Satan uses words and false teachings to lead believers and unbelievers away from God. He plants ideas that oppose the goodness of God and traps people into doing "his will" (v. 26). In the coming week, ask the Holy Spirit to help you speak only words that glorify God and help others to find Jesus. Next week we will concentrate on the terrible godlessness that will be prevalent in the world in the last days before the Second Coming.*

Notes on 2 Timothy 2:14–26

Summary: Paul's warnings in 2:11–13 about perseverance and not disowning the Lord lead straight back to the problem of the false teachers in the Ephesian church, which he addresses in this passage and the next.

2:14 *Remind them of these things.* Timothy's first task is to keep people in touch with the truth of the Gospel (which is summarized in 2:11–13). The verb tense indicates that this is something he will have to do over and over again. *fight about words.* Literally, "word battle." This lies at the heart of the false teaching. *ruin of the hearers.* Such quibbling over words has no good result.

2:15 Having defined the problem with the false teachers, Paul contrasts the ministry of Timothy. *approved to God.* Literally, "one who has stood the test"; a word used to describe gold or silver that had been purified in fire, or a stone that was cut without a flaw (which is examined and then pronounced fit to be used in a building). *a worker.* The picture is of a farm laborer who has done a good job and is therefore not afraid to show his boss what he has done. *correctly teaching the word of truth.* In contrast to the false teachers and their "word battles," Timothy is called upon to teach and preach the Gospel correctly. The phrase "word of truth" refers not to Scripture specifically, but to the Gospel message as a whole.

2:16 greater measure of godlessness. Paul indulges in a bit of irony suggesting that such speculation does promote growth, but in the wrong direction.

2:17 gangrene. A disease that "gnaws away" at healthy tissue, causing its decay. Likewise, false teaching eats away like a cankerous sore at the healthy life in a church. **Hymenaeus and Philetus.** Paul names two of the false teachers. Hymenaeus has been a real problem. Paul had mentioned him in 1 Timothy 1:20 as one he had "delivered to Satan." It appears he is still at work "overturning the faith of some" (v. 18). Why has Paul's excommunication failed to stop Hymenaeus?

2:18 the resurrection has already taken place. They were probably teaching that the resurrection of believers had already taken place in a spiritual (or mystical) sense, perhaps at the time of baptism (1 Cor. 15:12; 2 Thess. 2:2). This undermined the hope for a bodily resurrection on the Last Day (1 Cor. 15).

2:19 The faithfulness of the few is not the last word. As in verse 13, it is the faithfulness of God that is the final truth. **solid foundation.** Paul is probably referring to the unshakable core of genuine Christians at Ephesus. **having this inscription.** Paul has in mind the practice of placing an inscription on the foundation stone of a building to indicate the purpose of the building or who the owner of the building is.

2:21 It might be expected Paul's point would be that those Christians who have followed the false teachers are like wood and clay vessels, while those who have remained true to the Gospel are like the gold and silver vessels. His actual point (which he makes in this verse) is that Christians must cleanse themselves from false teaching. **purifies himself.** This phrase was used to describe ritual cleaning of dishes.

2:22 Flee/pursue. He is to avoid evil desires while striving for positive virtues. **youthful passions.** Paul has in mind the impatience and arrogance of self-assertive youth, who love novelty and indulge in argument for the sake of argument.

2:23 foolish and ignorant disputes. He is to avoid the kind of uninstructed theorizing that characterizes the ideas of the false teachers (1 Tim. 1:7). Debate about these ideas does not produce truth, only "quarrels."

2:24 Instead of quarreling, the Christian is to be "gentle," articulate ("able to teach") and "patient." **The Lord's slave.** Paul often uses the word "slave" to refer to those who are active in ministry.

2:25 Despite their error, his opponents are to be treated well. This is not to say that error is tolerated. The whole tone of the letter moves in the opposite direction. But Timothy is not to indulge in mean-spirited quarreling over truth. **repentance.** A change of mind. The image is of individuals who have been walking in one direction (in this case, away from God's truth) who have come to their senses, seen their error and decided to turn around and go in the opposite direction (toward God's truth). Repentance is a gift of God. **to know the truth.** This is the issue. Those who follow the teaching of the erring teachers are not walking in the way of the Lord and so need to repent, turn around and start walking in the truth.

2:26 come to their senses. This lies at the heart of "repentance." It is like coming out of a drunken fog into clear-headedness (the Greek verb means literally, "return to sobriety"). **escape the Devil's trap.** In fact, they have been ensnared by the Devil. As Paul pointed out in 1 Timothy 4:1, the source of their erroneous ideas is Satan himself.

Godlessness

Scripture 2 Timothy 3:1–9

LAST WEEK *"But avoid irreverent, empty speech, for this will produce an even greater measure of godlessness" (2:16). Last week Paul focused once again on how Satan was working through the false teachers to lead people away from the truth. We were reminded of the damage that words can do in our relationships with others and with God. This week Paul uses the example of these false teachers to highlight the evil that will come on the earth in the days preceding Jesus' second coming.*

 Ice-Breaker Connect With Your Group (15 minutes)

Sniper shootings, child abductions, violence in the schools—these are just a few examples of the godlessness we hear in the news every day. It's almost as if Paul had already heard one of our newscasts when he wrote today's passage. Take turns sharing your thoughts and experiences with disobedience and godlessness.

Leader
Choose one, two or all three Ice-Breaker questions, depending on your group's needs.

1. When you were growing up, what happened to you if you talked back to your parents?

   ○ I didn't.
   ○ I was grounded.
   ○ I had difficulty sitting down for a couple of days.
   ○ Usually nothing.
   ○ I got the silent treatment.
   ○ They yelled at me.
   ○ It was a constant battle.
   ○ Other _____.

2. When you were in high school, were there students who were a bad influence? What advice did your parents give you about these kids?

○ We were all angels.
○ My parents didn't know.
○ They wanted to meet my friends.
○ They told me to get new friends.
○ We had long talks.
○ My parents were my best friends.
○ What do you mean?
○ Other _____.

3. Where were you when the events of 9/11/01 happened? How did you react?

 Bible Study Read Scripture and Discuss (30 minutes)

In today's passage, Paul warns Timothy to avoid godless people, protecting his doctrine and life closely. In graphic description he gives the characteristics and practices of the first-century pagan society. The same characteristics and practices found in these "teachers" will be seen just before the Second Coming. Read 2 Timothy 3:1–9 and note Paul's concern for Timothy.

Leader
Select three members of the group ahead of time to read aloud the Scripture passage. Then discuss the Questions for Interaction, dividing into subgroups of three to six.

Godlessness

Reader One: 3 But know this: difficult times will come in the last days. [2]For people will be lovers of self,

Reader Two: lovers of money,

Reader Three: boastful,

Reader Two: proud,

Reader Three: blasphemers,

Reader Two: disobedient to parents,

Reader Three: ungrateful,

Reader Two: unholy,

Reader Three: [3]unloving,

Reader Two: irreconcilable,

Reader Three: slanderers,

Reader One: without self-control, brutal, without love for what is good,

Reader Two: ⁴traitors, reckless, conceited, lovers of pleasure rather than lovers of God, ⁵holding to the form of religion but denying its power.

Reader Three: Avoid these people!

Reader One: ⁶For among them are those who worm their way into households and capture idle women burdened down with sins, led along by a variety of passions, ⁷always learning

Reader Two: and never able to come to a knowledge of the truth. ⁸Just as Jannes and Jambres resisted Moses, so these also resist the truth, men who are corrupt in mind, worthless in regard to the faith.

Reader Three: ⁹But they will not make further progress, for their lack of understanding will be clear to all, as theirs was also.

2 Timothy 3:1–9

Questions for Interaction

1. Which of the following characteristics do you think causes the most problems in our society?

   ○ Conceit.
   ○ Anger.
   ○ Disobedience.
   ○ Dishonesty.
   ○ Slandering others.
   ○ Not caring about other's feelings.
   ○ No self-control.
   ○ Hate.
   ○ Loving money more than people.
   ○ Addictive behavor.
   ○ Other _____.

2. Do you think the culture in Paul's day was better or worse than today?

3. Of all the sins Paul lists, which one is the root of all the others?

Leader
Refer to the Summary and Study Notes at the end of this session as needed. If 30 minutes is not enough time to answer all of the questions in this section, conclude the Bible Study by answering questions 6 and 7.

4. What does it mean in verse 5 that they have a form of godliness but deny its power? When have you gone through the motions in your spiritual life without having a growing relationship with God? What happened?

5. According to verses 6–9, what is the character, danger and fate of these false teachers?

6. How do you respond to evildoers? Do you actively reach out to "sinners," or passively withdraw into a safe haven?

7. Is there any godlessness in your life today that needs to be corrected? What is it? What do you need to do?

   ○ Influence of the world.
   ○ Focus on material things.
   ○ Personal sin.
   ○ Lack of complete integrity.
   ○ Distance from God.
   ○ Estranged relationships.
   ○ Anger.
   ○ Insensitivity.
   ○ Other _____.

Going Deeper   If your group has time and/or wants a challenge, go on to this question.

8. How would you talk to someone about Christ who is "always learning and never able to come to a knowledge of the truth" (v. 7)? Is it helpful to get into long discussions and debates? Why or why not?

Caring Time Apply the Lesson and Pray for One Another (15 minutes)

Prayer can help us face any challenge that comes from living in a god-less society. Let's take some time to pray together and share our hopes and dreams.

1. As you look back over your life, what brings you the most sense of satisfaction and accomplishment?

2. As you look forward to the future, what do you want to accomplish with your life?

3. What challenge are you facing in the coming week that we can pray for?

Leader
Following the Caring Time, discuss with your group how they would like to celebrate the last session next week. Also, discuss the possibility of splitting into two groups or continuing together with another study.

NEXT WEEK *Today we were given another warning by Paul to beware of those who live godless lives, yet profess to be Christians. We were reminded to be protective of our faith and lifestyle, as we live in a secular and sinful society. In the coming week, take some time to reflect on your lifestyle and ask the Holy Spirit for discernment on things you should change. Next week we will conclude our study of 1 and 2 Timothy. We will focus on Paul's final words to Timothy, encouraging him to remember all he has learned and experienced as Paul's spiritual son.*

Notes on 2 Timothy 3:1–9

Summary: Paul places the false teachers in the context of the last days as an example of the evil that will come upon the world in the days prior to Jesus' second coming. Jewish tradition had long taught that there would be terrible times in the days just prior to the establishment of God's kingdom (Dan. 12:1; Mark 13:3–23; 2 Peter 3:3).

3:2 *people.* Although he casts this list into general terms ("people"), Paul implies that these vices characterize (at least in part) the false teachers. ***lovers of self.*** The moment a person makes his or her own will and desires to be the center of life, divine and human relationships become very difficult. ***lovers of money.*** The path is short from love of self to love of money. Self-interest leads to self-indulgence. ***boastful, proud.*** These two terms are connected. The first refers to outward expressions of unrealistic pride and the second to an inner attitude of superiority. These words can also be translated as "braggart" and "arrogant." These terms have already been applied to the false teachers (1 Tim. 1:7; 6:4). ***disobedient to parents.*** Both Greeks and Jews considered duty to parents obligatory. ***ungrateful.*** To be "ungrateful" is to refuse to honor the debt one owes to others. ***unholy.*** Such a person violates the unwritten laws that stand at the core of life.

3:3 *unloving.* This refers to the lack of natural, human affection. ***irreconcilable.*** Such a person finds it impossible to be reconciled to others. This sort of person is harsh and often bitter. ***without self-control.*** This is the person who is a slave to a habit or desire. ***brutal.*** This word

denotes a savagery that has neither sensitiveness nor sympathy. ***without love for what is good.*** Such people have lost their taste for good things and good people. They are content with the tawdry, and they find no pleasure in the company of those who are decent.

3:4 *traitors.* A traitor is a person willing to betray others for his or her own gain. This word was used of Judas in Luke 6:16. ***reckless.*** This is to be swept along by impulse or passion into bad decisions. ***conceited.*** Such people are swollen with pride at the sense of their own importance.

3:5 *holding to the form of religion.* The final item on the list points straight at the false teachers. They liked certain outward expressions of religion: the fasting and other forms of asceticism, the debate about religious ideas. But they missed out on the real "power" of God by substituting an outward religiosity for the inner reality of God. ***Avoid these people!*** Although he is to be kind to them (2:24–25), on an official level Timothy is to shun these teachers and their false doctrine.

3:6 *capture.* This verb can mean to take captive by misleading or deceiving. *idle women.* Paul uses a somewhat contemptuous diminutive form of "women" meaning "silly" or "foolish." *variety of passions.* There may have been some sort of sexual involvement between the false teachers and the women they influenced.

3:7 The women were given "religious training" of the worst kind, destined to feed their curiosity but not bring them to the freedom of the Gospel.

3:8 *Jannes and Jambres.* These are Pharaoh's magicians, who by means of their secret arts duplicated the miracles of Moses and Aaron. Although the names of Egyptian magicians are not given in the Old Testament text (Ex. 7:11–12,22; 8:7), by Paul's time tradition held that they were a pair of brothers with these names. They opposed the truth that Moses spoke in the same way the false teachers oppose the truth of the Gospel. *corrupt in mind.* As he has done before (1 Tim. 6:5), Paul asserts that far from being wise teachers with special insights into religious truth, the minds of these men have ceased to function.

3:9 Paul ends by pointing out that none of this will get these false teachers very far "because everyone will see how stupid they are" (TEV). In the end, they will be exposed for what they really are.

Paul's Final Words

Scripture 2 Timothy 3:10–4:8

LAST WEEK *In last week's session, Paul highlighted the evil that will precede the Second Coming to serve as a backdrop for his final words to the young Timothy. We were reminded how we must love those who are godless, but at the same time be protective of our own faith and lifestyle. Today we will conclude this study of 1 and 2 Timothy with a look at Paul's life and ministry, and how he wants Timothy to carry that ministry on when he's gone.*

 Ice-Breaker Connect With Your Group (15 minutes)

We have probably all been privileged at some point to have a mentor or teacher that had a life-changing effect on the direction we took in life. Paul was certainly that person to Timothy. Take turns sharing about some of these special people in your life.

Leader
Begin this final session with a word of prayer and thanksgiving for this time together. Choose one or two Ice-Breaker questions to discuss.

1. In high school, what subject did your favorite teacher teach?

    ○ Math.
    ○ English.
    ○ Science.
    ○ Political Science.
    ○ History.
    ○ Physical Education.
    ○ Other _____.
    Why was that teacher your favorite?

2. How old were you when you started learning the Bible? Who taught you?

3. What is some of the best advice that your parents have given you?

Bible Study Read Scripture and Discuss (30 minutes)

Leader
Select two members of the group ahead of time to read aloud the Scripture passage. Then discuss the Questions for Interaction, dividing into subgroups of three to six.

In this passage, Paul tells the story of his life and ministry. He then instructs Timothy to be faithful and continue the work that he has begun. Read 2 Timothy 3:10–4:8 and note the passion Paul has for the Word of God.

Paul's Final Words

Reader One: ¹⁰But you have followed my teaching, conduct, purpose, faith, patience, love, and endurance, ¹¹along with the persecutions and sufferings that came to me in Antioch, Iconium, and Lystra. What persecutions I endured! Yet the Lord rescued me from them all. ¹²In fact, all those who want to live a godly life in Christ Jesus will be persecuted. ¹³Evil people and imposters will become worse, deceiving and being deceived.

Reader Two: ¹⁴But as for you, continue in what you have learned and firmly believed, knowing those from whom you learned, ¹⁵and that from childhood you have known the sacred Scriptures, which are able to instruct you for salvation through faith in Christ Jesus. ¹⁶All Scripture is inspired by God and is profitable for teaching, for rebuking, for correcting, for training in righteousness, ¹⁷so that the man of God may be complete, equipped for every good work.

Reader One: 4 Before God and Christ Jesus, who is going to judge the living and the dead, and by His appearing and His kingdom, I solemnly charge you:

Reader Two: ²proclaim the message; persist in it whether convenient or not; rebuke, correct, and encourage with great patience and teaching.

Reader One: ³For the time will come when they will not tolerate sound doctrine, but according to their own desires, will accumulate teachers for themselves because they have an itch to hear something new. ⁴They will turn away from hearing the truth and will turn aside to myths. ⁵But as for you, keep a clear head about everything, endure hardship, do the work of an evangelist, fulfill your ministry.

Reader Two: ⁶For I am already being poured out as a drink offering, and the time for my departure is close. ⁷I have fought the good fight, I have finished the race, I have kept the faith. ⁸In the future, there is reserved for me the crown of righteousness, which the Lord, the righteous Judge, will give me on that day, and not only to me, but to all those who have loved His appearing.

2 Timothy 3:10–4:8

Questions for Interaction

1. What is the significance of Paul recalling the tough times that he and Timothy had together? What memories of tough times do you recall in your life?

   ○ As a child we were poor.
   ○ The other children didn't like me.
   ○ Home life was turbulent.
   ○ I was terrible in school.
   ○ Finances have always been hard.
   ○ I haven't found a satisfying job.
   ○ Bad boss.
   ○ Disappointing marriage.
   ○ Other _____.

Leader
Refer to the Summary and Study Notes at the end of this session as needed. If 30 minutes is not enough time to answer all of the questions in this section, conclude the Bible Study by answering questions 7 and 8.

2. Is persecution necessarily a result of godliness? Why or why not?

3. What does Paul say about where Scripture comes from (3:16)? What is significant about this truth?

4. Of all the purposes of Scripture listed in verse 16, how has Scripture helped you the most?

   ○ Teaching me truth.
   ○ Revealing errors in my life.
   ○ Helping me to measure my life.
   ○ Instructing me how to live.
   ○ Equipping me to do ministry.
   ○ Other _____.

5. Timothy's Ministry (4:1–5): What nine orders does Paul earnestly charge Timothy to carry out?

6. Paul's Ministry (4:6–8): In the conclusion to this letter—the last recorded message Paul wrote—how does the apostle sum up his life and ministry?

7. Your Life: How do the words of Paul challenge your life?

8. Your Ministry: How does this passage (or study) challenge your ministry? What is God asking you to do next?

9. Why did Paul and the early Christians think that the Second Coming was imminent? Why do you think Jesus has not returned yet?

Caring Time Apply the Lesson and Pray for One
Another (15 minutes)

Even as we face persecution, danger and discouragement, the life and ministry of Paul encourages us to run and fight to win. The powerful weapon that God has given to us for the contest is prayer. Let's spend time in prayer now, asking God to give each one of us the strength and support to go out and share Christ with others.

Leader
Conclude this final Caring Time by praying for each group member and asking for God's blessing in any plans to start a new group or to continue studying together.

1. Comparing your spiritual life to a race, where are you?

    ○ Just getting out of the blocks.
    ○ Really hitting my stride.
    ○ Nearing the finish line.
    ○ Tired out.
    ○ Other _____.

2. What will you remember most about this group?

3. How can the group pray for you in the coming weeks?

WHAT'S NEXT? *Today we saw the importance of passing the baton of the Gospel to men and women who are approved by God. It is crucial that all of us do our part to tell the world about the tremendous sacrifice of Jesus. In the coming weeks, ask the Holy Spirit to give you boldness in sharing your faith.*

Summary: This is a long "charge" to Timothy by which Paul concludes his comments to his "son in the faith."

3:10 *followed.* Literally, "to follow alongside." By this term Paul is urging Timothy to remember all he learned from him in the course of their travels and ministry together (2:2). This is especially important now, since Paul has come to realize that his own ministry is at an end. *my teaching.* This is the first of nine characteristics of Paul's life and ministry that Timothy is asked to note and reproduce. These nine make up a sort of "virtue list" that stands in sharp contrast to the "vice list" in 3:2–5 (2 Cor. 6:4–10). It is not by accident that Paul begins this list with "teaching." False teaching is at the root of the problem with the religious charlatans who are operating in their midst. Timothy must, above all, teach apostolic doctrine accurately. *conduct.* Closely following on the heels of good doctrine is a positive lifestyle. The false teachers lived in ways quite different from the Christian way of life. *purpose.* The motivation for Paul's ministry arose out of his single-minded devotion to Christ (Phil. 1:21–26).

3:11 that came to me. Each incident occurred on Paul's first missionary journey, culminating in his stoning while in Lystra (Timothy's hometown). By selecting these particular incidents, Paul is reminding Timothy of the fact that even at the start of his Christian life, he knew it involved suffering. *Yet the Lord rescued me.* Paul encourages Timothy (who will have suffering of his own, as Paul notes in 3:12) by the fact that God rescued him from death in each of these instances.

3:12 To be in union with Christ Jesus is to be persecuted. It is that straightforward.

3:13 Ironically, this is not the case for "evil men." They do not live godly lives and the implication is that they thus avoid persecution. *impostors.* This word originally meant a "sorcerer." It came to mean a "swindler" or "cheat."

3:14 *continue in what you have learned.* This is Paul's only command in this paragraph (3:10–17), and as such defines his key point. *those from whom you learned.* Those who taught Timothy were reliable people whom he knew well, unlike the charlatans who seek to worm their way into one's confidence.

3:15 *sacred Scriptures.* This means literally, "the Sacred Writings" and is a technical term for the Old Testament. *instruct you for salvation through faith in Christ Jesus.* The Old Testament Scriptures lead one to salvation; i.e., to an understanding of God's saving purpose. However, as Paul is quick to note here, salvation is not found in the Scriptures per se. Salvation comes through Christ Jesus, the one to whom Scripture points.

3:16 *All Scripture is inspired by God.* Scripture has a divine origin. It comes from God. *is profitable for.* By means of two contrasting pairs of phrases, Paul names four ministry tasks in which Scripture plays a vital part. *teaching.* Scripture is the source of what Timothy teaches, in contrast to the speculative nature of the erring teachers' doctrine. *rebuking.* Not only does Scripture teach that which is true, it also reveals that which is in error. Thus, Timothy can use Scripture to expose the fallacy of the false teachers. *correcting.* Scripture also defines how to live. It is thus a measuring stick against which to assess behavior and change what is found wanting. *training in righteousness.* This is the positive side of "correcting." Scripture provides instructions in how one ought to live (and not just in how one ought not to live).

3:17 *the man of God.* This may be a general term for every Christian, or it may refer specifically to ministers, whose task is, under the authority of Scripture, to teach and refute, to reform and discipline.

4:1 The basis of his charge is the second coming of Christ when all will be judged and his kingdom will be established in visible form.

4:2 *proclaim the message.* Above all else, Timothy is to proclaim the message of the Gospel. This is the main command and controls the next four. *persist in it whether convenient or not.*

Probably Paul is encouraging Timothy to keep on preaching whether his hearers find it convenient or not, though he may be urging Timothy to continue with this task whether or not it is convenient to him. *rebuke, correct, and encourage.* In preaching the Gospel he is to "correct" those who are in error, "rebuke" them if they fail to heed his correction, and "encourage" or "urge" them all to respond.

4:5 Paul ends his charge with four more imperatives that reinforce what he has already said to Timothy. *keep a clear head.* Literally, "stay sober" when those around you follow the desire of their "itching ears."